the LAW *of* *Happiness*

DR. HENRY CLOUD

the

LAW

of

Happiness

How Spiritual Wisdom and Modern Science Can Change Your Life

HOWARD BOOKS
A DIVISION OF SIMON & SCHUSTER, INC.

NEW YORK NASHVILLE LONDON TORONTO SYDNEY NEW DELHI

Howard Books
A Division of Simon & Schuster, Inc.
1230 Avenue of the Americas
New York, NY 10020

First Howard Books trade paper edition January 2012

HOWARD and colophon are trademarks of Simon & Schuster, Inc.

For information about special discounts for bulk purchases, please contact Simon & Schuster Special Sales
at 1-866-506-1949 or business@simonandschuster.com.

The Simon & Schuster Speakers Bureau can bring authors to your live event.
For more information or to book an event, contact the Simon & Schuster Speakers Bureau
at 1-866-248-3049 or visit our website at www.simonspeakers.com.

Designed by Ruth Lee-Mui

Manufactured in the United States of America

10 9 8 7 6

The Library of Congress has cataloged the hardcover edition as follows:

Cloud, Henry.
The law of happiness : how spiritual wisdom and modern science can change your life / Henry Cloud.
    p. cm.
Includes bibliographical references.
1. Happiness—Religious aspects—Christianity. 2. Happiness. I. Title.
BV4647.J68C56 2011
248.4—dc22
2010014185
ISBN 978-1-4391-8246-8
ISBN 978-1-4391-8055-6 (ebook)

To my daughters, Olivia and Lucy.
The happiness you bring cannot be measured.

CONTENTS

CONTENTS

INTRODUCTION

*F*ROM THE LAW OF ATTRACTION TO THE LAW OF HAPPINESS

A FEW YEARS ago, a book called *The Secret*, by Rhonda Byrne, took the world by storm with the claim that the real secret to life and happiness lies in a force called the Law of Attraction. In fact, the book's premise, as you may recall, was that the entire universe is governed by that one principle. Byrne's claim was that the universe responds to your thoughts and that you attract happiness to yourself by the power of what you think. If you think positive thoughts, the universe responds to your thoughts by bringing positive outcomes to you, and if you think negative thoughts, your outcomes will be negative. People by the millions responded to the idea that this one law was the secret to happiness and all they desired in life. And, as a psychologist and performance coach, I can certainly tell you that people who think positively have much better outcomes than negative thinkers. For sure.

While Byrne's book deals with concepts that interface with spirituality, it also brings up a lot of questions about how the Law of Attraction interfaces with more traditional views of spirituality, God, and the like. The first book in this series, *The Secret Things of God*, examined where those principles agreed with traditional faith, where they disagreed, and also what clinical experience and research say about the same issues. It was a really meaningful project for me, personally, and many readers responded as well.

So that brought us to the question of "what next"? What other topics of personal well-being also interface with spirituality and spiritual wisdom? When my editor asked me that question and what I would like to write about, the answer was immediate. "I want to write about happiness," I said.

"Happiness? Why happiness?" she asked.

I explained that the field of psychology in the last several years has been actively exploring what is referred to as "positive psychology." A number of years ago, Martin Seligman (then president of the American Psychological Association) and others championed the message that while psychology had made great strides in its studies on the "negative" side of life—such as depression, trauma, anxiety—it had spent relatively little time studying the "up" side of life. Topics such as happiness, well-being, strengths, etc., had not gained the same amount of attention, especially from scientific research. Researchers began to soundly answer that call.

The result has been an enormous amount of empirical studies that have shed substantial light on questions such as: "Where does happiness come from?" "Can people increase their happiness?" "Is it under our control?" And the good news is that research has actually produced a lot of answers. We now know, not just from experience, but also from scientific data, a lot about the sources of happiness and the lifestyles and practices that actually produce overall well-being.

I would have enjoyed writing about this happiness research and how it applies to life, but that has been done already by others. I did not feel the need to add to the list of good books out there. But I was drawn to writing a book on happiness for The Secret Things of God series because of what had happened to me as I was investigating the field of positive psychology.

As the profession was churning out more and more information on the positive side of life, learning was a lot of fun, and the data clearly resonated with my own experience, both professionally and personally. I had seen firsthand the truths that the research was revealing, so I loved what I was studying. But for me, it was much more than that.

It was a spiritual journey as well. *As I was reading the research findings, I felt like I was reading the Bible.* It was as if someone took the data and laid the Bible right on top of it and the fit was perfect. Basically, over and over, the robust findings of the research were the same as the ancient spiritual wisdom found in the Scriptures. I saw Moses, Solomon, Jesus, and Paul as I read study after study, which were proving that happiness and fulfillment is not found in our circumstances, our bank accounts, our material possessions, or achievements. Instead, what the research revealed was that happiness comes largely from how we live our lives and into which activities we decide to invest our hearts, minds, souls, and strength.

So that is why I wanted to write this book on happiness in a series of books about how faith integrates with life. Just as the Bible has a lot to say about "positive thinking" and the Law of Attraction, it has even more to say about happiness and fulfillment. In fact, one of my favorite words that we hear over and over in the Bible is the Hebrew word *shalom,* which among other things implies peace, happiness, well-being, wholeness, completeness, and welfare—most of what we mean when we say we want to be "happy." In short, we can be assured that the Creator has always been interested in our happiness and well-being.

But further, he is also interested that we know how to find shalom: *by investing our lives in the ways that he designed life to be lived.* And that was where I was so impacted by the research. It was literally proving through science that the path to happiness is the path that God has been telling us to walk for a long time. Happiness comes as a by-product of the "life well lived." And that is what brought me to the title, *The Law of Happiness:* I wanted to show the two things that the research has shown me.

Number one, that happiness can be found and there are principles and practices that reveal that. And number two, those principles and practices, the "law of happiness," are the ones that God has given all along in his "law," the Scriptures. From the Torah, which means "instruction," through the rest of the Bible, he has shown us the "law of happiness." And now science has verified what the Bible has said all along. For me, that was a really cool thing to behold, and I hope it is for you as well—that you further experience how faith and science interact.

So join me as we take a look at what science reveals and what spiritual instruction has shown us about where happiness comes from. *Shalom.*

The Science of Happiness

MY CO-HOST ON our radio show, *New Life Live!*, lit up with
enthusiasm when I pulled my minicomputer out before the
show one day. "I am so excited," he exclaimed. "I just got
one of those and can't wait to use it. People tell me that what
they can do is incredible!"

"What do you mean 'can't wait to use it?'" I asked. "If
you have it, why aren't you using it?"

"Something is wrong with it, and I have an appointment
to take it in. I brought it home, and it wouldn't turn on," he
said, "so, I have to get it fixed."

"That's strange," I said. "It is unusual for them to ship
one that won't even boot up. What did you try?"

"Well, I hit the buttons there on the bottom, and clicked

it a bunch, and kept trying over and over, but it never would do anything," he explained.

"That is so weird," I said. "But why were you hitting those buttons? Those are the mouse clickers. Did you hit this one up on the corner?"

"What is that? I didn't see that one," he said as he peered over my screen.

"Watch this," I said.

As I hit the power button, the familiar blue screen came up, the sound effects chimed in, and my friend stared in amazement. "What did you do?" he queried.

"I turned it on," I replied. "It works better when you do that."

So, what does my colleague's computer have to do with happiness? Turns out, a lot.

Here is what the scientific research is finding about happiness: *we are wired to experience happiness, but we keep hitting the wrong buttons in our efforts to turn our happiness on.*

As I mentioned earlier, for more than a hundred years, psychology has often been interested in happiness only in its absence. The interest has focused more on our pain, hurt, depression, and anxiety: "Why do we suffer, and what can the doctor do about it?" And, as research validates, psychology has done quite a good job. We know how to treat depression, anxiety, addictions, and other issues well. The results are promising. And if you are experiencing any of those pains, there is help for you. I strongly encourage you to seek out competent psychological and psychiatric help. In our discussion about happiness, I do not want to seem to ignore the very real pains in life.

But, what about the upside of life? Is there more to life than not being depressed or unhappy? What scientific research has found is that, just like computers are designed to work when properly turned on, humans are wired in such a way that when properly "turned on," they get happier. Their brains begin to secrete chemicals that make them feel better, their bodies get healthier, they make more money, their relationships improve, their marriages are more fulfilling, they live longer, and their overall sense of well-being and happiness gets better. And what is amazing is that we now have a lot of documentation to show exactly where the power buttons are and how to turn them on.

THE LAW OF HAPPINESS

Humans are wired in such a way that when properly "turned on," they get happier.

PUSHING THE WRONG BUTTONS

Unfortunately, we often don't know where the power buttons are, so we keep pushing the wrong ones, hoping that we are just one click away from happiness. People watch talk shows on TV and think the experts being interviewed have the answers. We think that if we try this or that particular diet or do what this magazine article says or buy the secret that this infomercial is selling us, we will get to the land of happiness. We are just one click away from having it all come together . . . or are we?

We fall prey to thinking things like:

- If I could just make a little more money, then I would be happy.
- If I could just find that special someone and get married, then I would be happy.
- If I could get that promotion, then I would be happy.

- If I could finally own a home, then I would be happy.
- If I could move and live in a different city, then I would be happy.
- If I could get that new model (of whatever), then I would be happy.
- If I just could get my _____ degree, then I would be happy.
- If I could lose twenty pounds, then I would be happy.
- If I were beautiful, then I would be happy.
- If we could move to that neighborhood, then I would be happy.
- If I were rich, then I would be happy.
- If I were famous, then I would be happy.

Research and spiritual wisdom both reveal that while many of these items certainly have value, none can bring much *sustainable* happiness. And that is what I mean by "pushing the wrong button." While most of what we need to feel better is readily available to us, we often don't know where to find the correct buttons, and we continue to look to the wrong buttons and hope they will work.

PATHS TO UNSUSTAINABLE HAPPINESS

There are at least three reasons that the new house, the new job, the new relationship, the bigger bank account, or any of the other things on the list will not make us happy.

Reason Number One: Our External Circumstances Do Not Have the Inherent Power to Bring Us Happiness

If you look at the list above, you'll see that all of these de-sires—as well as many others—are circumstantial. They are "states" within which we find ourselves, like rich or poor, degreed or not, renting or owning, skinny or fat. These states can change at any given time in our lives. But most of all, they are "outside us." What has the research into happiness shown us about our circumstances? The answer is surprising, especially since we live in a culture that is obsessed with the list above and others like it. Here is the finding: *Circumstances account for only about 10 percent of our happiness.*[1]

It is true that when you get a promotion or that new car you have wanted or most anything else on the list, you will feel a sense of happiness for a little while. But what science has found is that you might think you are going to be a lot happier than you actually are after you get what you want. Circumstantial things or events have the power to make us happier—but only a little bit—and as we shall see in a moment, only for a little while. As my father used to tell me, "Son, money can't buy happiness. But it can buy you a big red Cadillac to go look for it in."

In other words, money is not a bad thing, nor are nice houses. But don't bank on it as the answer to happiness. I do remember when my dad got his first Cadillac—and it was a happy day for him—but as I have come to understand from my professional life and experience, the happiness that *he brought* to that day from living a certain kind of life was much more powerful than that car ever could be. All the car did was give him a comfortable ride to his various life activities, which were already producing his real and lasting happiness and continued to do so for most of his ninety-four years.

The fact that our circumstances have limited power to make us happy has been documented in the research; but if you think about it for a minute, you already know this from your observations while standing at the check-out counter at any grocery store. Look at the magazine headlines and you will see rich, beautiful, accomplished, famous, slim, and successful people, but with all sorts of unhappiness, from relational turmoil to drug abuse and overdose, and even suicide.

If circumstantial things could bring us lasting happiness, we would not be seeing those sad headlines. And the flip side is this: if circumstantial things and events are the sources of happiness, why are there so many happy people who *don't* have many of those things going for them? In fact, studies have shown that the happiness levels between rich people and average-income people is not that different. The findings say that once a certain safety and sustenance level has been reached, more money is not going to bring much more happiness.[2]

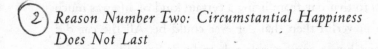

Reason Number Two: Circumstantial Happiness Does Not Last

Psychological research has shown something else about "getting" or "achieving" some external, circumstantial state as the path to happiness: *It does not last.* It has a short shelf life. So, not only do our circumstances and achievements account for only a small percentage of our happiness, but even what they are able to contribute evaporates pretty quickly. Why?

It seems that there is some sort of "set point" to our level of happiness that we carry around, almost like a thermostat.[3] Let's say your set point from factors other than circumstances is at 70. Then you get that new house, and you jump up to

80 or, for a day, to what feels like 100! This happens, for instance, when people first fall in love with the persons of their dreams. They may even exceed 100 in that initial state. (That explains a lot of crazy behavior.) But whether it is the house, the raise, or the relationship, what research has shown us is that we come back down to the place we were before. We return to our set point. This is called the "hedonic treadmill." This is why, as common sense will tell you, you can look back at things you thought you would "just die for," and now they are stored in the garage and you don't care much for them anymore. Their power has gone away. Compare children on Christmas morning to those same children a few months later when the toys they were so excited to find under the tree lie around no longer used.

I remember when I was in graduate school, working hard to get a doctoral degree. I thought that when I got that degree, life would change. I thought of all the things I could do with it and all the doors that would open up for me. When I got the degree, I remember the initial sense of accomplishment when I went to the hospital to work and they called me "Doctor." It felt nice . . . for a few days. But the truth is, I haven't thought about it much since then. I was still *me* whether I was called Henry or Dr. Cloud, and my happiness had more to do with whether I was practicing the laws of happiness than with the fact I had a degree. The conclusion: *The happiness that external things or circumstances bring does not last.*

Reason Number Three: When We Are Pursuing the Things That Don't Have the Power to Make Us Happy, We Are Ignoring the Ones That Do

This is the flip side of the first reason about circumstantial answers to happiness. The list does not have the power to make you happy, and as you are focused on those kinds of answers, you will not be focused on the things that actually *will* make you happy. It is a little like dieting. If all you are eating is junk food, not only is it not helping (and probably hurting), but at the same time you are not getting the nourishment your body needs that would change your whole metabolism. Just like your body needs certain nutrients to make it healthy, your heart, mind, and soul need certain practices to make them happy.

When my two little girls are headed off to play soccer, and all they want for breakfast is pancakes and syrup, they have two problems. What *they* want to eat is not going to help them play soccer (in fact they will have a big sugar crash in the second half of the game), *and if it was left up to them, they* would not be eating the good proteins and complex carbs that will sustain them throughout the glucose curve. And the data are in . . . there are happiness "foods" available that will help us in known sets of activities. But if our focus is on the wrong things, we will not be doing the right ones.

THE MATHEMATICAL MAKEUP OF HAPPINESS

A great body of research has shown us what goes into happiness. Here is the math:

As mentioned earlier, at any given moment, *circumstances may be contributing about 10 percent or so to your happiness.* If life is going well, you get a lift, and if life circumstances are not so great (other than times of great tragedy or trauma, which can bring a season of great pain), you get a little downturn. This is the first 10 percent of why you feel like you do.

The next factor comes from *your internal makeup, which is probably composed of genetic, temperament, and constitutional factors.* This seems to account for about 50 percent of your happiness level.[4] Go to any infant nursery, and you can almost see the different levels at work. Some babies are happy with the world, and others are going to have to work at it a little bit more! Look at children even a little older and you can see their natural dispositions even more. They are all different, and so are we. You do bring some genetic components and factors into life, which contribute to your moods and sense of well-being.

And now for the very good news:

The rest of what goes into your happiness comes from things that are directly under your control: your behaviors, thoughts, and intentional practices in your life. The things you do "on purpose." What you give your attention to, what you give your energy to, and what goes on inside of you have the power to make you happy. These are factors that you and only you control.[5]

THE CHALLENGE AND THE WARNING

So, that leaves us all with a decision. Or better yet, an entire lifetime of decisions. Moment by moment, day by day, year by year, decade by decade, choices create a direction. Or deciding on a direction will dictate each choice. And that direction of how we invest our lives is under our control. We all have the choice to invest ourselves in living in ways that produce happiness, or continuing down a road that experience and science has shown will never fulfill us.

But it does bring up a question. If spending all of our time pursuing the 10 percent (as if it is going to be the key to happiness) does not work, then why in the world do we do it? Why do we think that "if I only had . . . then I would be happy?" Take Rachel, for example.

Rachel was single and was convinced that her life would not begin until she was married. She had so many good things going on in her work and other areas of her life, but to her, being married was her holy grail. In her mind, as long as she was not married, she was in a sense waiting for life to begin.

"Why do you think you won't be happy until you are married?" I asked.

"It has just always been the way it's supposed to be," she said. "You get out of school, and then you find a mate, settle down, and raise a family. It is my dream and always has been. I will be devastated if I don't get married."

"'Devastated' is a word I think of when someone goes through a tragedy," I said. "Would not being married really be a *tragedy*?"

"Isn't it a tragedy to have a life with no happiness?" she asked.

You can see her problem. Tragedy equals not having happiness, but happiness comes only from marriage, so no marriage equals no happiness and a tragic life.

"Do you think that every person who is single is miserable?" I asked. "Or do you think there are any happy ones?"

"I don't know," she said. "I guess there are some happy ones."

"I promise there are. So, what do you do with that?" I asked.

She did not have an answer. But it made her look at her life: if other people can be happy and not married, then apparently marriage is not the key to happiness.

I told her that the reality was this: happy single people who get married are happy married people. Unhappy single people who get married become unhappy married people. So her task was not to focus on getting married, but to focus on becoming a happy person in whatever state she found herself. She was surprised to know that the research shows little difference in the happiness between singles and those who are married. Obviously this happiness is coming from something other than their marital status, as many single people are happy too.

As a psychologist, I could have also told her of so many people I have talked to who had it all, marriage included, and yet were still unhappy. They had achieved fame, riches, family, career, and all that people think will bring them the happiness they desire, yet those things had not delivered what the people thought they would.

But we often are tempted to still believe the "if only." We think that if our outside circumstances would change, we would be happy. Not true, says both the research and the experience of a lot of people who finally found what they were seeking and yet are still searching. So why do we fall prey?

It is human nature, pure and simple. In my view, it's best explained in the story of the Garden of Eden. And although it was written thousands of years ago, the basic spiritual dynamics are the ones that we live every day and that also govern our pursuit of happiness. The story of these dynamics could have happened yesterday, and actually does each day, in all of our lives.

The events go like this: God created a good life, a beautiful garden with lots of trees that represent all of the good stuff. And he gave an instruction. His commandment was "to eat from any tree in the garden." In other words, "I have created some great stuff here. Have a good time, eat, and be satisfied with what I have given you." He didn't go into all the fine details like the fact that he had also carefully placed taste buds in the design of the human tongue to fully appreciate the fruits, or biochemical releases in their brains that make their hearts happy when they do certain things. And he usually doesn't explain all the whys to us. He just basically said, "Here is life. Go for it. Enjoy. Trust me, it will work." (I am sure that some of those trees represent the great golf courses of the world. After all, August National is in the Peach State, right?)

And, he had one warning. Adam and Eve were not to eat of the tree of the "knowledge of good and evil." "For when you eat of it you will surely die." What was that warning? It was basically the warning to keep from playing God and thinking that you can be like him, knowing what is good and what isn't. Just trust him to do his job of knowing what is good for us, and then do your job of enjoying it.

We all know what happened from there. The serpent came and tempted them, saying that they could be like God and really know it all. They could know "good from evil." He told them to forget following God's direction and design, and go their own way, apart from God. So they did, and became separated from God and his ways, as well as separated from being able to enjoy all the fruits of the good life that God had created. Here is the lesson: *In going for what they thought was going to make them happy, they lost the things that really do.*

The result was that they found themselves in a very unhappy state, disconnected, and ashamed. Not a good day. But to me the lesson of the story is so much what all of the happiness research shows us as well.

When we are not eating the fruits of the good life that God has created, and think that we know what is going to satisfy us instead, we will continue to go hungry. Unsatisfied. Unhappy. Unfulfilled. But because we do not see how we get seduced into thinking the human race can play God and figure it out on our own, we continue to not see the trees with the good fruits that are available right in front of us. We fall prey to the temptations of advertising, the media, culture, materialism, sensuality, or faulty comparisons with others, among other things. But, as the story reveals, they are all the same. *They are but one tree, no matter what the temptation.* It is the temptation to not live life in accord with the design that God wired into all of life, not investing in the real trees that are fruitful.

And I don't know about you, but for me, following spiritual truths is always hard. I know God's principles and yet I hear the Serpent say, "But . . . you are only one more gadget away from contentment," or other such lies. So, it is nice to remind myself that this is not just theology or Sunday School. It is also empirical data. Science says that when we do the activities that the Bible tells us to do, we are better off for it.

So, that is our challenge. Live life investing in the ways that it was designed to be lived. When we do, as we shall see, happiness will follow. Let's now move into seeing thirteen ways of happiness where God and science agree.

2

HAPPY PEOPLE ARE GIVERS

WHEN MY OLDER daughter, Olivia, was about three or four, she attended a half-day preschool a few days a week. She loved it and was making lots of friends. One day, before I took her, for some reason we got into a conversation about sharing. We talked about how you can share all sorts of things with others, from love to helping someone, to sharing cookies and toys. I suggested that when she was at school that day, she find someone and share something with her. I thought it was one of those normal on-the-run father-daughter talks. I didn't think much about it.

Later, though, something happened that I will never forget. I picked her up from preschool, and as we were walking around the neighborhood, she began to tell me about her day. I asked her about all her activities, and she told me they had made some cookies and how much she loved them. Then she told me she saw that one of the kids didn't have any, for some reason, so she walked over and gave some of her cookies to him. I thought that was nice but not earth shattering. She had shared things before. What she said next, however, was.

"Daddy, something happened. I don't know what it is," she said as she gave me a serious look.

"What, Livi? What happened," I asked.

"Well, when I gave Brandon the cookies, I felt something in here. Right here." She immediately pointed to her little chest. "It felt really warm in here. What was that?" she asked.

When I heard that, I actually felt like I was going to break apart in tears, but I managed to hold them back. "That was love, Livi. That is what you feel inside when you give things to people. It makes you feel nice and warm inside."

"It feels really good," she said. "I want to do that some more. I like it."

I will never forget that moment. So many different thoughts and feelings were going on inside of me, from just the sheer beauty of it all to appreciation of her heart, and other feelings. But one of the strongest feelings I had was something like, "I don't think I have to worry about her future happiness. She has found the key."

IT IS MORE BLESSED TO GIVE THAN TO RECEIVE

One of the strongest findings of the happiness and well-being research over the years is that people who are givers, those who serve others and are altruistic, are much happier than the ones who don't. And some have even shown how the brain is wired to produce that feeling "in here" that my daughter was having. For example, neuroscientists Jorge Moll and Jordan Grafman from the National Institutes of Health showed that pleasure centers of the brain, the ones that respond to food and sex, also light up when people think of giving to others.[1] God has actually hooked your brain up in a way that makes you feel good when you give. In a way, that is the central message of this book: we are wired for a happy life—sometimes we just have to learn what that happy life looks like.

While there may be some activities in life that are in question, giving to others is not one of them. Showing acts of kindness and being altruistic are not activities we have to wonder about. If you want to increase your happiness, spend some of your heart, mind, and soul—even your money—on others. Research has shown that when people spend money on others or on charity versus themselves, the money spent on others is the money that returns happiness. Giving actually makes people happier than spending money on themselves.[2] Giving to others makes you healthier as well as happier. It is good for your mood, your soul, and your body. Studies have shown that giving, helping, and serving is related to mental health, and those who help others have less stress, anxiety, and depression.[3]

There are many other findings, much too numerous to go into here, but suffice it to say, giving and serving are good for you. As the old saying goes, "the research is in." But do we really need research to tell us? My daughter didn't, even at age three or four. Her research went on in her own heart. She *felt* it. "It feels warm in here." Could there be a better barometer of happiness than one's own heart?

My hunch is that you know this. Think back to a significant relationship in your life, a person who caused you to expand your heart and open up to a higher place where you wanted to give of yourself. Do you remember that feeling? But past that, do you remember your actions? What did you do? You gave. You went out of your way. You sacrificed. And what did you feel when you did? "Warm inside." That is what we are talking about.

Wotdn't the light bulb come on

22

THE LIFE OF A GIVER

But the question is, how do we make that feeling stick around? How does it become not just an isolated occurrence here and there but a way of life? Here are some tips.

(1) *First, give out of faith.* What I mean by that is that God has told us to give, and when we do what he says, we are acting in faith even when it does not give us a warm feeling in our hearts. Maybe it even hurts a little. Sometimes we don't feel like giving, and we have to be told to do it. Just like Olivia had to be nudged by her dad to give and to share, sometimes we have to be nudged too. And God nudges us in many places in the Bible. For example, he tells us to give out of gratitude and faith, and to give to him the *first* part of what we have:

> *A tithe of everything from the land,*
> *whether grain from the soil or fruit from the trees,*
> *belongs to the LORD; it is holy to the LORD.*[4]

> *Celebrate the Feast of Harvest with the*
> *firstfruits of the crops you sow in your field.*[5]

One of the best happiness structures in life, I believe, is the principle of giving to God, and giving to him first. I learned it from my parents, who learned it from the Bible. When I was young, probably four or five years old, they gave me a dollar a week every Sunday morning for my allowance, with specific instructions: First, take a dime of it to church and give it to God to show him thanks. Second, take another dime and put it in your piggy bank. Third, do what you want with the rest. Now, the percentages have changed over the years, but not the order. God first, save second, spend third. The Bible's teaching on giving is the foundation for financial happiness, but going into that whole topic is more than we have time for here. The emphasis here is that giving to God first gets the whole system going down a certain path. This is done out of faith and gratitude, as we obey this part of his ways. And, like other aspects of the life of faith, give it time. Watch for the fruit of increasing happiness to grow in various ways as you continue to give.

THE LAW OF HAPPINESS

One of the best happiness structures in life is giving to God, and giving to him first.

2 *Second, give out of empathy.* Look around you at who is hurting. Who needs help? Who can you identify with, either imagining what their situation must be like or truly knowing because you have suffered the same way? Let your compassion be your guide, and it will connect you to life in a way that you never imagined.

3 *Third, give out of your whole life,* not just your material resources. God tells us that money is just a tool; it is not what our life consists of.[6] Our real life comes from giving of ourselves. When you give your time, your energy, your heart, and your mind to others, you will reap the benefits way past the giving of your money. Do volunteer work. Take food to a family with a newborn whose mom has no time to prepare meals. Babysit for a single mother to give her an afternoon or evening off. Visit the sick in the hospital. Write notes to people to encourage them. Lead a small group in your church to support people in need. Give your time at a homeless shelter.

My parents lived to be ninety-two and almost ninety-four; both died last year within a few months of each other. When I attended their funerals, I saw the reality of Jesus' words that a person's life is not their possessions but their investments of themselves. For those days, I could see the fruit of their lives and will never forget it. Many, many people came to pay respects to a couple who had served their community together for the sixty-six years they were married. They had tutored children, supported poor churches, delivered meals to people who could not leave their houses, volunteered at charities, and on and on. One woman told me that when she and her husband were a young couple and had just moved to town with no friends or family, my parents showed up at their house to help get them plugged in. She said that being "adopted" by them is what gave them a start in a new town and made all the difference. In those few days of their respective funerals and visitations, I was so impacted by what a life of giving produces.

But what also stood out was remembering back to when they were doing those things. I never saw them as "on a mission" or doing anything that anyone else would even know about. To me, they were just living another day, and another day meant that someone was going to be given to in some form or fashion. To them, that was just life. And I remember their being fulfilled for a long, long time.

So don't think that you have to be a missionary in some faraway land. Take soup to a sick friend or cookies to the office. Just think, a little each and every day, of what you can add to someone else. Your life will change over time, little by little, as you give of yourself.

4 *Fourth, give in a structured way.* What I mean is this: just as God told us to give of the "firstfruits" and gave us a structure for giving to him, we need to think of giving of our time and resources in a structured fashion. Here is the truth about life: whatever resources you do not set aside and protect will get spent on their own. You must decide first what you want to give and put it on the calendar and in the budget. Otherwise, it will get spent on other things.

So in the beginning of the year, months, or weeks, set aside some time for service. Decide as an individual or as a family that you are going to donate X amount of your days this year to volunteer, or X amount of hours a month, and put it on the calendar. Do the same for your money. If there is more left over and God blesses you in that way, then you can give more. But make a commitment first that you stick to, and that way it will be sure to happen.

5 *Fifth, make sure that you are giving "freely."* Listen to this passage from the New Testament:

> *Remember this:*
> *Whoever sows sparingly will also reap sparingly,*

and whoever sows generously will also reap generously.
Each man should give what he has decided in his heart to give,
not reluctantly or under compulsion,
for God loves a cheerful giver.[7]

The above verse talks about three kinds of giving. Some people give "reluctantly"—this is the kind of giving that results from manipulation and pressure from the outside. Don't let people push you past where you want to go. Others give "under compulsion"—or as a result of their own guilt, or pressure from the inside. But the kind of giving that God wants is that which each person decides in his own heart and gives freely and cheerfully.

This is why those who give past where they should, such as codependents, often get burned out; and why some care-givers suffer too, as they overextend themselves. If you are in that position, establish some boundaries so that your giving does not lead to burnout. That is something the Bible teaches over and over. God is cool with your not "giving too much." Having limits does not mean you are selfish. Selfish is when we don't give at all. Giving past your emotional resources will not lead to happiness; rather, it sometimes leads to unhappiness. As Moses was told by his father-in-law, you will "wear yourselves out."[8]

THE LAW OF HAPPINESS

Giving past your emotional resources will not lead to happiness,
but sometimes to unhappiness.

Sixth, give past your comfort level at times. I know I just said not to give past your resources or under pressure, and I meant what I said for those situations. But the truth is that healthy giving is like a muscle. We have to use it and pick up more and more weights to make it stronger. Some people only give when it feels convenient or they are in the mood. But Jesus told us that when we give, our hearts follow our giving. "For where your treasure is, there your heart will be also."[9] Giving itself can help to form us and what we care about. So, at times, take the big gulp and give past your comfort level, and you might find that comfort and more happiness will follow.

Seventh, make it relational. Sometimes you will give on your own and that is wonderful. In fact, a lot of giving is about giving in ways that no one will even know. As Jesus said, not even your right hand should know what your left hand is doing. But, at other times, it is helpful to be part of a giving community. Join a service club or group or put one together. Find a buddy to do volunteer work with. Do it as a family with your spouse and kids. There are many ways to give in relational teams, but do it. It will be fun to share together, and you will mutually motivate each other. As the Bible says, "Let us consider how we may spur one another on toward love and good deeds."[10] Help each other become helpers, and we all grow in the process.

And last, give to those who don't deserve it. Jesus told us to give to our enemies and to those who won't return the favor.

> *Love your enemies, do good to them,*
> *and lend to them without expecting to get*
> *anything back. Then your reward will be great,*
> *and you will be sons of the Most High,*
> *because he is kind to the ungrateful and wicked.*[11]

If we are only giving to get or giving because someone is deserving, that is not the whole picture of giving. Giving is about giving, period. There is something about doing good for those who don't do good toward you that takes giving to a whole different level, the level at which God gives. He is "kind to the ungrateful and wicked." If you want to feel all of what giving has to offer, give in these difficult economic times as well. And when you do, you will sometimes be surprised that your act of undeserved kindness does exactly what God's gifts do: it may melt the heart of an ungrateful and unkind person and help her turn around in some way. Gifts change people, and if you practice goodness to people who are "not good," you may see them wake up.

So, in sum, as Jesus said, "it is more blessed to give than to receive." It is true, and the research has proven it in many ways. The giving life is the happy life and the best gift that we can receive.

$\mathcal{H}$APPY PEOPLE ARE NOT LAZY
ABOUT HAPPINESS

AS A KID, I remember watching an episode of the comedy show *Hee Haw* where two of the farmer types were lying on the ground back to back, chewing on pieces of hay and just watching time go by. One of them said something to the other about a beautiful woman who was walking by. He was struck by how pretty she was and described her to his friend.

The second one, not moving or turning around, responded something like this: "Wow . . . wish I was looking that way."

The funny interchange was fueled by one simple fact:

he was just too lazy to turn around and enjoy the view. It is a funny scene, but when you take the same attitude and behavior out of a comedic skit and see it in the real, day-to-day lives of people, it is not a funny reality at all. The truth is that many unhappy people desire to be happy, but when potential happiness walks by each and every day, they "wish they were looking that way" but find themselves not turning around to join happiness when they could.

Now, before I get into the dynamics of laziness and happiness, let me be crystal clear about one thing: sometimes clinical conditions, such as severe depression, actually do immobilize people. The inability to get going is part of the illness itself. If you are one of those people and would love to be able to take part in life and work toward feeling better but are immobilized and literally do not have the energy to do so because of deep depression or other clinical issues, you are *not* lazy. You have an illness and need medical treatment, and I encourage you to get help immediately.

What I am referring to in this chapter is the kind of person who is able to do what would help make him happy, but for whatever reason, he doesn't do it. As Proverbs 26:15 states, "The sluggard buries his hand in the dish; he is too lazy to bring it back to his mouth." The "dish" is there and available, but the person is not taking advantage of the "food" that is waiting. He is not doing the things that could actually bring him the happiness he desires.

Contrast that attitude and behavior with that of happy people. Those who wake up in the morning and say, "Good morning, Lord!" instead of "Good Lord, morning," usually do not find themselves in that place by happenstance. They find themselves there by exercising their God-given energy, investing their time, moment by moment and day after day, in the activities of building a life that is fulfilling and meaningful. In effect, they are living out the created order itself. God designed us to be, in his image, persons who use their hearts, minds, souls, and strength to create and invest themselves in producing life. They build relationships and use their talents and abilities to achieve things, and God wants us to do the same. He wants us to be active toward life, not passive.

> *My dear friends, as you have always obeyed*
> *—not only in my presence, but now much more in my absence*
> *—continue to work out your salvation with fear and trembling,*
> *for it is God who works in you to will and to act*
> *according to his good purpose.*[1]

Happy people are active, not passive, in their pursuit of life. If you look at some of the activities that research has proven produces happiness, you'll see that it takes effort and investment. For example, happy people invest their time:

- Building deep relationships and community: they belong to support groups, participate in Bible studies, or have structured times of getting together with friends and family and nurturing those relationships.
- Being involved in growth activities: they see a coach or a counselor or attend some kind of growth group.
- Pursuing goals: they have physical, financial, vocational, avocational, or other goals they're working toward.
- Serving others: they have found meaningful ways to give of their time and talents.
- Nurturing a spiritual life: they devote time to spiritual activities, such as prayer, meditation, Bible study, retreats, and so forth.
- Exercising and staying healthy: they have some sort of routine that they follow to stay active and pursue a healthy lifestyle.
- Practicing gratitude: they regularly express gratitude to God and others.

- Pursuing activities they love: they find their passions and pursue them.
- Stretching themselves: they look for activities and goals that push them to be all they can be.
- Resolving pain and conflicts: whether in relationships or in their own souls, happy people do not avoid problems but do what is necessary to heal them.

These are just a few examples of the kinds of activities we are examining throughout this book, but they show that happiness does not just fall out of the sky and land in people's laps. Happy people engage life and pursue their dreams.

My experience has been that when people get a wake-up call about their level of happiness in life, their first realization is that they are responsible for their own happiness, and their second realization is that they will need to pursue certain activities. I have seen many people who, having been stuck for years, finally "get it," wake up, and say, "I do not have to live like this. I am going to do something about my life." Then they get busy, and a year later, I hardly recognize them.

But for that to happen, you have to find the "push." You have to overcome the entropy and lack of movement that has dominated you for so long. You have to "do something." So how will you do that?

Other than those who might be clinically depressed or suffering from a real illness of some sort, there are two broad types of people reading this book. The first is the type who, upon reading what I have written so far, gets up and gets moving. She says, "This makes sense. What have I been doing?" So she'll call a support group, join Weight Watchers, sign up for that community college class, take up rock climbing, call a therapist, or do whatever she has been avoiding that takes a little effort. If that is you, God bless you. You are on your way.

The second type is the one who reads this and finds that it resonates, wants to pursue change, but will probably not do anything. Is there hope for him? Absolutely, but not on his own. If this is you, you need two things: *energy and structure.* You have shown how, when left to your own devices, you are not going to self-motivate and do not have the needed discipline. So you have to find energy and structure from the outside.

I suggest that you get a buddy, an accountability partner, a group, a therapist, a class, a trainer, a coach, or whatever it is going to take to get you moving and continuing to move. At this point in your life, if you do not have outside structure and someone motivating you, you will slip back into passivity. But think about it this way: if to get active enough to get someone to push you or to join a class is being as active as you can be, *that is great.* They can help you from there. That is all you have to do, but *you* have to do it. Otherwise, you are in danger of continuing to do nothing and being lazy about your happiness.

As you read this book, look at all the ingredients we are talking about and find your own plan as to how you can put them into practice. A little bit each day, morsel by morsel, will help you to grow and get on a path that will result in the fruit of happiness. Just the simple act of picking up the phone and calling a friend to go to lunch could have a measurable effect on your brain chemistry. You won't hit the happy meter in one day by any one activity, but that is not how happy people operate anyway. Do the little things day-to-day that make people happy, and over time you will find yourself to be one of those kinds of people: happy and invested in life.

> *We do not want you to become lazy,*
> *but to imitate those who through faith and patience*
> *inherit what has been promised.*[2]

I love this verse. It gives one more example of the created order, the way God set up the universe. He makes promises about life, and then he expects us to do our part and not be lazy. He promised the children of Israel a "promised land," but they had to go and possess it. They had to fight a lot of battles to get there. And, little by little, they did. "Imitate those who through faith and patience inherit what has been promised." God has promised you abundant life, but he has not promised you an abundant life with no effort. Work on your happiness, take responsibility for it, get moving. Work out your salvation with fear and trembling, for it is God who is working within you. He is doing his part; now you have to do yours. Don't be lazy!

Since I write books, people often come up to me and say, "I would love to write a book. I have been wanting to write one for a long time. I already know what I want to write about."

"How long have you been wanting to do this?" I ask.

"Oh, for years and years," they respond.

"Well, why don't you do it?" I ask.

"Oh, I just don't have the time," they say. "I have a job and cannot just be a writer."

"I have a job too," I tell them. "I have to write in my spare time. It has only been recently that I have been able to set aside time specifically for writing. But my first twenty books or so, I had to do it when I could find a moment."

Most often they just look at me. Then I tell them, "You will find time to do what you want to do."

I love the story of John Grisham. He was an attorney and a state legislator but always wanted to be an author. Obviously he was busy, full-time and more. But with a dream of writing a novel, he got up a little earlier each day and wrote one page. Within a few years, he had *A Time to Kill: A Novel.* He has sold more than 100 million books since then, but it all started by not being too lazy to write just one page a day. Get moving toward the activities that are going to make you fulfilled and happy. One page or one call at a time.

$\mathcal{H}$APPY PEOPLE DON'T WAIT FOR "SOMEDAY"

I REMEMBER A friend of mine in graduate school whom I was always trying to get to go play golf or take a ski trip with a bunch of us or do other fun things. He was a good guy and someone we would have enjoyed being around. But every time I would ask, he would say something like, "I would love to, but I have to . . ." and go on to explain how he had to finish whatever he was working on first, and "then . . ." he would be able to have time to do some of those fun activities we were trying to recruit him into doing.

It was either a paper or a semester project that he had to finish before he could have fun, or he had to take another course, or, or, or. I finally quit asking, thinking, *Getting a doctorate must be totally consuming for him, and maybe when he gets finished, he will be normal.*

It just so happened that after graduate school he ended up settling in a town not too far from me, so I would run into him from time to time. Several times, when a group of us was going to do something fun, like take a ski weekend or go on a weekend trip to Mexico, we would invite him. I remember thinking, *He is out of school now, so maybe he will be normal.* But each time, he would decline. At that point, he would say, "I have to finish my hours for licensure first, and then I will be able to do those kinds of things. I look forward to it, but I have to get this done first."

You know where this is heading. He got his license, and we invited him some more. And he would say, "I want to, but now that I am licensed, I have to work on setting up and building my practice first. Then, when I am all set up, I will be able to do some of these things with you guys." I gave up on his becoming normal.

What I realized was that it was not the paper that had to be finished or the degree or the dissertation or the internship or the license. None of these was in the way of his having a life. It was him. He was in the way. His mentality was in the way. He had a way of thinking that basically went,

When _____ happens, I will have a life. Fill in the blank, but _____ never happens. It was always something, because it was him. He had a "future" mind-set about happiness.

Earlier, we talked about the kind of thinking that goes, *If only I had _____,* which pictures some circumstance as the source of happiness. It is the "what" mistake—thinking "what" will make me happy is a particular circumstance of some sort. The thinking mistake we are looking at in this chapter is the "when" mistake. It is a way of thinking that says happiness is always later in the timeline, and that happiness will come "when" a particular something is done or achieved. It is the inability to enjoy the now and the thinking that says the only happy time is in the future.

- When I get my degree, I will be able to enjoy life.
- When we finally get moved in, we will be able to enjoy the new town.
- When I get through this project, I will be able to enjoy myself again.
- When I get finished with my training, then I will love life.

Each of the above statements is an example of how some people feel that happiness is on some sort of timeline and depends on a later event. It cannot happen now, because there is a missing piece that has not occurred yet. But in reality, people who think this way do not magically become happy "when" the "whatever" it is happens. They just transfer that mind-set to the next "when."

HAPPY IN THE NOW

Happy people are happy "now." Because they practice all the ingredients we are looking at, they are never dependent on a someday or a tomorrow to be the key to their well-being. They are fulfilled before that upcoming event ever takes place. They are happy "now."

What gives them this ability? Several ingredients, but first and foremost it is a spiritual discipline of living in the now. Listen to how Jesus puts it:

> *Do not worry about tomorrow,*
> *for tomorrow will worry about itself.*
> *Each day has enough trouble of its own.*[1]

While the Bible certainly tells us to plan for the future, it also tells us to live in the present, each and every day. Today, or better yet, this moment, is all there is or all there ever will be. You can never experience tomorrow, ever. When it gets here, it will be just another moment like today, and if you do not have the spiritual discipline of experiencing the "now moment," when it gets here, you will miss the tomorrow that you are waiting on right now. Just like my friend in graduate school . . . tomorrow never comes. As someone once said, "today is the tomorrow you worried about yesterday."

THE LAW OF HAPPINESS

Today, or better yet, this moment, is all there is or all there ever will be.

Research has shown that people's ability to focus on the moments they are experiencing right now, the joys and pleasures of the present, actually make them happier and less stressed and depressed. Happiness researcher Sonja Lyubomirsky, one of the leading happiness scientists, puts it this way: "People who are inclined to savor were found to be more self-confident, extraverted, and gratified and less hopeless and neurotic. . . . Those skilled at capturing the joy of the present moment—hanging on to good feelings, appreciating good things—are less likely to experience depression, stress, guilt, and shame."

Lyubomirsky goes on to cite how people were given the exercise to savor two pleasurable experiences a day, even mundane experiences, and others were asked to take a few minutes to relish normal experiences and write about how they experienced them. Both had improvements to their moods and depression.[2]

Some systems of therapy that have strong empirical proof behind them are built around helping people to develop "mindfulness," which is the ability to focus on one's experience and be with it, right in the now. One continuing education class for psychologists that I took spent an entire hour getting us to try to "experience the moments that we were experiencing" right then and there and to describe them to one another. It was amazing how difficult that was for a room full of PhDs who have spent most of their lives "training for the future." It was an art that many of them reported as having lost along the way with so much left-brained schooling.

But, as research proves, when psychologists can get their clients to do just that, to be "in the now" with their lives, feelings, and experiences, their clinical symptoms of depression, stress, and other maladies improve.

Avoidance Coping Mechanism

Much of people's inability to live in the present results from their trying to live in the future to avoid what they are experiencing right now. They are like a hamster on a wheel, always trying to stay one step ahead of their feelings. The behavior is often a coping mechanism that was developed early in their lives to avoid painful feelings or to give them a feeling of control over environments that were painful or stressful. But the problem is that now the coping mechanism from the past works against them, creating more stress and keeping them from achieving happiness in their present lives. They take their pasts with them into the present and continue to re-create it. The human mind just does that.

"Trained" Stress Triggers

I was participating in a leadership event with former prime minister Tony Blair, and my task was to interview him about his experiences as a world leader. I was asking him about the mind-sets, pressures, stresses, and so forth—generally what the experience of that level of leadership was like. One story he told me was that at Prime Minister's Questions, which is a brutal question-and-answer session that Parliament holds at regular times, he would always notice his internal stress level rising as that hour approached on the schedule. It happened like clockwork in his internal system.

But the interesting thing was, he told me, that even years after being in office, when that hour rolls around, he can still feel his stress level go up. He got conditioned to being on alert, even though he is no longer having to field those questions in that stressful format. His mind still gets ready. When it does that, he probably is not completely "in the moment" wherever he finds himself at that time, until he refocuses and reminds himself that he is no longer there, but "here."

Think about that in terms of yourself. Your mind may have also been trained to be "on guard" for what is coming and to live more there than where you are right now. In the meantime, you may be missing your God-purposed life because of an old stress pattern.

Make the Most of the Current Opportunity

The Bible has some important things to say about living in "today," which is really all we have. Earlier, I quoted Jesus' teaching about not living in tomorrow, but being present in today. The book of Ecclesiastes says the same thing. It is a strong spiritual discipline taught throughout the Bible.

Here is how the apostle Paul put it:

> *Be very careful, then, how you live*
> *—not as unwise but as wise,*
> *making the most of every opportunity,*
> *because the days are evil.*[3]

Making the most of every opportunity means a lot of things, but one of them is making the most of the now, the moment. Think about the fact that if you are somewhere, that is your life. That is where you are, and that is the most important thing that could be happening right then, obviously, or you would be somewhere else. So live it. But to do that, you have to focus. It is a discipline.

I had to learn this as a writer. A book is a project that just does not go away until you finish it. So in a sense it is always hanging over your head until it is done. I enjoy writing, but it demands keeping to a timeline, which is sometimes not fun. Publishers require the book to be done by a certain date.

In writing season, I often feel the deadline pressure, even when I am doing something else. That pressure can take me out of the experience of whatever the something else might be. The most common scenario around which I had to develop spiritual discipline was time with my little girls when deadlines were looming. I love playing with them. The joy of spending moments playing games on the floor or walking to the park or engaging in other activities is the real essence of life. But those moments do not get me closer to meeting my writing deadline. So I would find myself not "being there" with my girls at times, worrying instead about what I was not getting done.

Then it occurred to me—*I am not writing; I am playing now. So stop writing while you are playing, Henry! Be here.* I had to learn to be present and embrace the experience of those hours, right where I was. To look into their eyes, feel the love welling up inside me as I got lost in the wonder of who they are and their personalities. No work task could come close to that for pure joy, I learned. I found that when I learned to be "there," "there" was awesome, and I found that I could be happy *even in deadline season!* That was huge for me.

What that experience did was carry over to a bigger lesson about life, as I rediscovered living in the moment in a lot of areas. But the area I'm most thankful for is the one involving my girls. I was in danger of one day watching them leave home and suddenly becoming aware that I had missed the joy, even though I had been there all along. Being there and not being there. I have to say it was one of the most important realizations I have ever had, and I hope you learn it as well. Living in the present will make your stress go down and your happiness go up. Even if the present is sad, to embrace those feelings is part of having them pass. Feelings that we avoid get stuck in our system and will return until we face them, so whether in good times or bad, the lesson is to be "in time." Be there, in the now.

THE LAW OF HAPPINESS

Living in the present will make your stress go down and your happiness go up.

SAVORING LIFE

The discipline of "savoring," as the researchers call it, is simply focusing on and fully tasting life—feeling your feelings, noticing what is around you, celebrating the good things that are before us each and every day. The Bible tells us to do this in many different places. Listen to Solomon speak of enjoying and savoring life:

> *There is nothing better for a man*
> *than to enjoy his work. . . . When God gives any man*
> *wealth and possessions, and enables him to*

enjoy them, to accept his lot and be happy in his work
—this is a gift of God . . . However many years a man may live,
let him enjoy them all.[4]

So how are you doing in regard to enjoying each moment and realizing that your moments and experiences make up your life? No matter what you are counting on happening "later" or what you're expecting to make you happy, the reality is that you are where you are now, and learning to savor the experiences you have now is a key skill in acquiring the happiness mind-set. Feeling appreciation, love, satisfaction, and so forth for all that you have and are experiencing now is where happiness is found, not in what is going to happen "when."

I have a friend who, in the financial meltdown of 2008, lost a literal fortune, millions and millions of dollars. He went into a depression that he could not get out of, as all he could think about was all the money he had lost and how long it would take him to "make it all back," as he put it, "if I ever can." He would just look at how far away that possibility seemed and see nothing but depressions ahead of him. He told me he was not able to get out of it.

We were having dinner, and he was telling me about how he felt his life was kind of over, in a way. This happened toward the end of the dinner, as I had been visiting with him, his wife, and his two children. Throughout most of the dinner, up until that point, we had been laughing and recalling lots of funny times and memories. Also, his kids had been very entertaining. We were having a wonderful time. But, as his attention turned toward the bigger picture of his losses, he got solemn as he described his life to me. After his description of how bad his life was, I asked him a question.

"So how is this moment, right now?"

"What do you mean?" he asked me, a bit puzzled.

"Say, in the last hour or so before we started talking about the future and the money, how have the moments been of this dinner?" I clarified.

"Uh . . . good, I mean, I've really had a good time," he said.

"Right," I echoed. "And that is my guess about your life. Your life is good, Rich. Very good, composed of many good moments like this. You loved the food, the laughs, getting a kick out of your kids and your wife, reminiscing with me over the great times we've had over the years. You told me you guys had a wonderful time today at the beach. If you think about most of the moments in your life, they are good.

"The things that truly give you joy and happiness—connecting with your wife, playing with your kids, spending

55

time with your friends, enjoying good food and a glass of wine—you still have. And, frankly, that is your life. Your life is happy.

"But your focus is not on your life. Instead, it is on whatever that money meant to you in some kind of way that has nothing to do with your life. And your obsession with a bank balance is keeping you from your real life, which you just said has had good times in it. Remember, Jesus said that your 'life' does not consist of your possessions.[5] Your life consists of the experiences that you have with the people you love and the matters of your heart, mind, and soul. Not some future bank balance that you will earn back "when." Your life is now, and it is still, in reality, just as good as it was when you had the money, in terms of the things that really matter. Your life is good, so grab it and you will be much happier," I said.

THE LAW OF HAPPINESS

Your life consists of the experiences that you have with the people you love and the matters of your heart, mind, and soul.

"I never thought about it like that," he said. I could actually see an opening in his eyes that looked like a light coming on. I hoped so.

So many times people miss the life that is right in front of them, which, if savored, would actually change their mood, outlook, physiology, stress level, and a host of other aspects of their well-being. But their focus is not on the moment right before them, but somewhere in the future set of "whens."

It is an old saying, but now science is proving it: "Stop and smell the roses" is more than a platitude. It is good psychological advice, and right from the mind of God. He created your senses and your ability to enjoy each moment. Take a warm bath and feel the water as it relaxes your muscles. Go on a walk and notice the beauty of the trees. Look into the face of a child and feel joy fill your soul. Experience the warm sun on your skin as you lie on the beach. Jump into the pool and notice the cool water enveloping you on a hot summer day. And then there is food . . . but this is not a chapter on my addictions. So let's just say that God has wired you to savor and enjoy life. As you do, your mood and outlook changes. Savoring life is a skill that will take some focus. But it is also one of his "ways" that we are to follow.

I remember once telling a couple who were having struggles to schedule a date night each week and go out. And I wanted them not to talk about problems on their date, but just to enjoy each other as they had in the good times. Immediately the wife rolled her eyes and shook her head no.

"Why not?" I asked.

"Because he will just be doing this," she said, while mimicking a person typing on a BlackBerry. "The whole dinner he will be checking e-mail and not talking. I will feel like I am there all by myself."

My heart sank for them. Here he was with a wonderful opportunity to connect with his wife, the one that Solomon says to "enjoy,"[6] and yet her experience has been that when he is with her, he is not savoring the moment. He is there and not there. And what he doesn't realize, as he checks one more e-mail about a deal that he thinks will make him happier "when" it happens, his happiness is sitting right across the table from him as he fails to savor the moment.

Recently I visited a friend at his lake house, and he gave me a tour. As we walked across the yard, he showed me the view across the glassy water toward the orange sunset. He pointed to the swing hanging from two old trees and said, "I am not a psychologist, but I do know this: no matter what is wrong with you, if you just sit on that swing right there, look at that sunset, reach out and hold the hand of someone you love, it will all get better. That's my psychology." He was a successful professional, and yet what mattered most in his life was available to anyone. I thought, *How many people on this lake do not have the capacity to enjoy it in the way that he just described?*

He had found true wealth, not in the fact that he had a house on a lake, but that he could savor the sunset and a connection with a loved one. That ability is what Jesus referred to as a person's "life," which did not consist of his possessions or something that was coming "when." It was right there and always available to him.

So if you want to improve your happiness, look at your orientation to the moments before you each and every day. Embrace them. Savor and celebrate the good things. Meditate on the experiences and memories that have meaning for you. Taste, touch, smell, feel, look at, and embrace each gaze, meal, walk, and every other activity that you do. If you do that, you will be living your life now and will not have to wait for "when" whatever comes that you think will make you happy. Now is the time.

$\mathcal{H}$APPY PEOPLE PURSUE GOALS

I WILL NEVER forget her face that Friday. But to get to that, we have to go back to the Sunday night before. I had just begun a weekly practice on Sunday nights with my daughters, who were six and eight at the time, where I sat them down and asked them for their stretch goals for the week. In other words, what were they going to do in the coming week that would stretch them past where they had been before, to be better and improve in some way?

This particular night was interesting because I was leaving town for the week and would return on Friday, so I told them I would be looking forward to seeing how they did while I was gone. When I asked them what they wanted to accomplish that week, my little one, Lucy, said

"Daddy, I am going to read ten books this week while you are gone!"

"Lucy, no," I said. "A goal has to be realistic. You are not going to read ten books, so pick a goal that you will actually do. How about five?" To fully understand this, you have to know that she was at that beginning stage of reading when it is a struggle, and she would often unplug when it got too hard. I saw five as an improbable goal at best, and ten as totally out of the question.

"No, Daddy. I want to read ten," she persisted.

"Lucy . . . no. Just do five so you can really do it. It will be fun," I pushed.

"Daddy, NO!" she pushed back. "I am going to read ten."

"Okay, great," I said, swallowing my angst that her failure would disappoint her and perhaps crush her goal orientation for life. One of the problems of being a psychologist parent is that you tend to project too much into the future. One misdeed on their parts, and I tend to see prison in their twenties. So I relented. "I can't wait to see!" I said, encouragingly . . . sort of.

I went on my trip, and on Friday night when I walked through the door, Lucy's sister, Olivia, ran up and screamed, "Dad! Lucy has something to tell you!"

"What is it?" I asked, wondering what was wrong.

"I READ FOURTEEN BOOKS!" Lucy exclaimed, face beaming and hardly able to contain herself.

"WHAT?" I asked, totally shocked. "FOURTEEN? OH MY GOSH! I can't believe it! That is awesome!"

From there we had a big celebration, and it was a real breakthrough for her. Now, a year later, she is thriving in her reading and enjoying it immensely. Not just because of that incident, certainly, as there has been other work to do. But it *definitely* was a turning point and something that we all can learn from—something that the research proves over and over: *setting and reaching goals is good for us.* The Bible puts it this way:

> *Hope deferred makes the heart sick,*
> *but desire fulfilled is a tree of life.*[1]

When we set goals and put legs to our desires and reach them, it definitely does do the heart good. A listless life that never strives to reach goals can feel lost. The research says that not only the attainment of our goals but also the pursuit brings joy along the way. As happiness researcher Sonja Lyubomirsky says, "People who strive for something personally significant, whether it's learning a new craft, changing careers, or raising moral children, are far happier than those who don't have strong dreams or aspirations. Find a happy person and you will find a project." Further, "it turns out that the process of working toward a goal, participating in a valued and challenging activity, is as important to well-being as its attainment."[2]

Indeed, as I found out later, Lucy was passionate all week long while I was away. She was getting up early to read, then structuring her time in the evening to get another book finished. She was on a mission, motivated and fulfilled along the way. It was not just about Friday. She was on fire all week long.

Not that an entire life can look like the sprint of that one week. Life is a marathon. But what we know about goals tells us that both the sprints of short-term goals and the marathon of a life spent pursuing longer-term goals and purposes contribute to satisfaction and well-being. They give us something to give ourselves to and invest our passions and strengths in. They help contribute to the "flow," which is a happiness factor in and of itself. They structure our lives and give them direction. They help order our time and energy. And a host of other benefits that contribute to a sense of well-being.

—NOT JUST ANY OLD GOAL WILL DO

Not too long after Lucy busted her goal and read so many books, I was out on a walk with my other daughter, Olivia, who was eight at the time. We were walking along, talking about various topics, when she said, "You know, Dad, I want to talk about this stretch goal thing."

"Yeah? What about it?" I asked, touched that it mattered to her enough to bring up.

"It's not working for me. I don't like it," she said.

"What? Why not?" I asked.

"Well, every week you ask us about our goals, and if we don't have one, you tell us to think of one," she said.

"Yeah . . . and?" I wondered, "What's the problem?"

"Well, that's not a goal. A goal is not something that you should have to think about. If it doesn't just come to mind right then, and you have to think about it, it can't be a goal. A goal has to be right there in your heart ready to come out," she said. "If I have to think about it, I don't want to do it."

Immediately my mind went to the research on goals and how the findings say that intrinsic goals are the ones we follow and complete and add meaning, and how externally imposed goals are not worth that much. In other words . . .

65

Olivia *was right.* Quickly, I scrambled, coming up with what I thought was a good answer on short notice.

"Well, that's not exactly right," I said.

"Why not?" she asked.

"Do you remember a few days ago when you came to me and said you were bored and I said you were responsible for your own fun? And so you went up to your room and went searching through that old trunk of toys. You found a bunch of old toys and used them to create a whole world, and you had a blast. You had a good time. Remember that?" I asked.

"Yeah, so?" she said, not budging.

"Well, your heart is like that treasure chest. Sometimes you don't know what is in there until you go digging a little bit. And then you'll find a treasure buried deep in your heart . . . a desire you didn't even know was there, and it becomes a goal. So that is why I ask you to think about it sometimes," I said, feeling like I had dodged a bullet.

She didn't immediately respond, walked several more steps, and then said with a sense of summary judgment, "Nope. That's still not a goal."

Oh well, I thought, can't win 'em all. But we are still doing stretch goals on Sundays.

THE LAW OF HAPPINESS

*Intrinsic goals are the ones we follow
and complete and that add meaning.*

You can be the judge whether or not a goal is still an intrinsic goal if it takes thought and soul searching. I believe it
is, as many times people are out of touch with their true desires, motivations, gifts, and directions. I think we evolve over
time . . . and perhaps when Olivia has more than eight years
to process life, she will join me in my opinion. But I think I
have both research and the Bible on my side.

First, research shows that intrinsic goals, ones that come
from who you truly are and are chosen by you as opposed to
being forced upon you from the outside, are the most powerful. Likewise, the Bible says we are not to chase pursuits that
are not congruent with who we are either. It tells us to not be
"conformed" to the world and its pressures, but to find our
true gifts and exercise them to the best of our ability.[3]

Choosing Goals That Fit

So grasp the goals that immediately jump out of your heart
and have been there for a long time, or do the digging into

your heart to find your true desires. Either way, get going. Make sure your goals are your own goals, not someone else's. I have the goal to finish this book, am having fun working on it, and know that I will feel satisfied in about another month when it is all done. That works. Following are some principles that can help you set goals:

Choose goals that fit your strengths and gifts. If I had the goal to win a Super Bowl, I would end up miserable. Just because we have a goal doesn't ensure happiness. That is why God tells us to make sure we are living the path that fits us.

Break your goals down into doable chunks. For example, in the writing of this book, I could *not* just sit down and write a book. I had to find out how many words it had to be and when it was due to the publisher, and I had to get on a schedule to write so many words a week between the start date and the deadline. So the big goal is made up of a lot of smaller goals, with weekly milestones.

Next, *your goals cannot conflict with each other.* Years ago I did an entire workshop, helping people decipher their goals and get the conflicts out of them. The results were that folks who had been stuck for a long time found themselves released to get moving, as the conflicts were removed. You can't, for example, reach two goals that are both vying for the same chunks of time. Or you can't reach one particular goal that someone disapproves of if you have another goal to make that same person happy. You have to pick one.

Also, *add some structure and support to your goals, and you will do better.* If you join a weight-loss group, for example, to get to your goal weight, a structured program will help you. If you get a personal trainer or join a class, you will experience forward momentum. The same is true for financial goals or any other kind. Structure is very important in making goals a reality, especially if you have trouble with self-discipline. If this is you, don't neglect the power of support. Social support in reaching goals has been shown to be of utmost importance. Use the buddy system. As Ecclesiastes says,

> *Two are better than one,*
>> *because they have a good return for their work:*
> *If one falls down,*
>> *his friend can help him up.*
> *But pity the man who falls*
>> *and has no one to help him up!*
> *Also, if two lie down together, they will keep warm.*
>> *But how can one keep warm alone?*
> *Though one may be overpowered,*
>> *two can defend themselves.*
> *A cord of three strands is not quickly broken.*[4]

Connected people do better in all aspects of life, especially in setting and reaching goals. Even for individual goals and pursuits, working with another person or a small group that supports your goals and can help you will drastically increase the odds of success. The other day a friend of mine asked my opinion about his weight problem. He said he could not keep it off, even though he lost it many times. He weighs about three hundred pounds.

THE LAW OF HAPPINESS

*Connected people do better in all aspects of life,
  especially in setting and reaching goals.*

I asked him how he had lost the weight each time, and he named several well-known programs, all of which include group meetings and support. I found it curious that he could not keep it off in that kind of structure, when he had been so successful at the beginning stages. So I asked further, "What did the group do when you would start to slide?"

"I didn't keep going to the groups," he said. "I am not much of a group person."

"I hate to tell you this," I told him, "but the research shows that the two go together. If you drop out, you are not as likely to be successful. It was working, as long as you were going to the meetings. But when you stopped going, you gained it back," I said. "You are proving the research."

"Here's the deal. I am not lecturing you about having to go or not go. I am just reporting to you the data. It is like gravity, neither good nor bad. You can take it or leave it, but the research shows that you will be way more likely to reach your goals with group support. That is just a neutral fact," I said.

All he could do was nod. You can't argue with data, you can only choose which side of it you are going to be on. Want to reach your goals? Find a buddy, or several.

Another way to reach your goals is to *find goals that are consistent with your values and the structure of your life, ones that give your life purpose and meaning.* The ones that mean something to you are the ones that are going to make you the happiest along the way.

And remember, the happiness is found not mostly in the finish line of your goal but in the journey itself, so *choose goals that call for you to love the work itself and that involve you in tasks you enjoy doing.*

If you want to get in shape but hate jogging, then ride a stationary bike while you watch your favorite DVDs. If you want to fight homelessness but are afraid to work in the inner city, join the fundraising arm of a local shelter and have a goal to bring in one hundred new donors. As much as is possible, enjoy the steps that get you to that finish line.

Certainly, you are not going to enjoy every minute of achieving any significant goal. Any goal worth its salt involves sacrifice. I heard an Olympic gold medalist interviewed about getting up at five o'clock every morning and getting into a cold pool to train; she said, "I hate it. I hate mornings, and I hate cold water." So nothing worth achieving is a cakewalk. But I am sure she loves swimming and loves competing in the Olympics. So, in those ways, she even enjoys getting up early in cold water, as it is part of the big picture. So be prepared for sacrifice, but find sacrifice that has love somewhere in it.

Big Picture and Small Picture

And remember, life is about the big picture and the small: life-goals, five-year goals, yearly goals, monthly, weekly, and daily goals. I love to not only think about the big picture in my life and work, but the small goals as well. For example, today, as I got set to write, I asked myself, *At the end of today, what will I consider a good day of writing?* I assigned a page number to that goal, and at the end of the day, bar interruptions, I will get there and be much happier than if I had floundered.

And that day will be added to other days that will give me a week's success, a month's success, and so on. Ultimately, I will reach the goal of finishing this book, and that itself will fit into my life goal and purpose of providing helpful information that will improve people's lives. (You can be the judge of whether this book is helpful to you.) But the big picture can't happen without the little, daily goals. They go together. You want to lose fifty pounds? Then have a little goal of going on a forty-five minute brisk walk every day. Little adds up.

Make your goals specific, measurable, attainable, realistic, and timely, commonly known as SMART goals. Dream big, but make that big dream something real that is able to be attained, measured, and can fit into the real world of time and deadlines. Real, attainable, and structural goals will engage you and help you feel successful along the way.

God made you like him, a person who is creative, has talents, brains, and abilities, and can see into a future that does not yet exist. Goals will help you bring all of those together. Create your dreams, large and small, and engage your talents and abilities to create the tomorrow that you envision. It will definitely add to your happiness.

$\mathcal{H}$APPY PEOPLE FULLY ENGAGE

HAVE YOU EVER had the experience of time just "flying by"? You are engaged in some activity, and you get so lost in the experience that you lose all track of time, to the point that at the end you say, "Where did the time go?" Or, have you had the opposite experience where you were so unengaged that it seemed like time was not moving at all? It just dragged and dragged, and you felt like you would never get out of "there?"

A minute is a minute, and an hour is an hour. Yet, at different times, with different people, and with different activities, one minute can feel very different from another and one hour from another. And in some instances, minutes can even feel like hours. Why is that? How can the same amount of time feel so different in different moments?

We do not know all the reasons—as time itself has its own mysteries—but research does tell us a few things, and one of them is exactly what the Bible tells us: *The engaged life is the good life.* over and over it tells us to do whatever we do with our whole heart.[1]

What does that mean? It means that when you are connected to what you are doing, you are a happier person and time just seems to disappear. If anything, you wish there were more of it, not less. And the opposite is true as well. The less engaged you are, the slower time seems to go by; you wish for something different to happen soon, yet it seems like it never will. (Why does twelfth-grade English class come to mind?)

The Bible calls this kind of full engagement being "wholehearted." Wholehearted participation means that you are really involved in what you are doing, and if you are, according to studies, you are going to be happier. You are "in it" with all of who you are.

One of the bodies of research on happiness focuses on this experience in depth and gives it the term "flow." It is the wholehearted involvement in an activity that takes us to another level of existence. A researcher named Mihály Csikszentmihalyi has done extensive work in this area and has isolated the conditions under which flow occurs. Flow is the name he gives to the experiences of people where "the sense of the duration of time is altered: hours pass by in minutes, and minutes can stretch out to seem like hours. The combination of all these elements causes a sense of deep enjoyment that is so rewarding people feel that expending a great deal of energy is worthwhile simply to be able to feel it."[2]

CONDITIONS NEEDED FOR FLOW TO HAPPEN

Flow doesn't just happen any old time. The conditions present when flow occurs, according to Csikszentmihalyi, are some combination of certain elements. For example, the activities we are doing must be both challenging and ones we have the ability to pull off. We must be focused and concentrate. We need to have clear goals, know what is expected, and know how we are doing. We need to be deeply involved and have some control over what we are doing. And we need to lose ourselves and a sense of time. The activity takes "all of us" and we're in the flow.

I am amazed at how those elements are prescribed throughout the Bible in the concepts of wholeheartedness, diligence, giftedness, self-control, and investment in meaningful activities. God does not want us wasting our time. He wants us investing our time in ways that make time itself go away. As I read the accounts of people in the flow experience, I always think that the timelessness they talk about happens because they have exited earthly experience and tasted a bit of eternity. Heaven knows no time, and when we are closest to heaven, we know no time either.

THE LAW OF HAPPINESS

As I read the accounts of people in the flow experience, it seems they have exited earthly experience and tasted a bit of eternity.

But to get there, to be that happy, requires that you involve yourself in activities you truly love and that you are developing the skills that will allow you to enjoy those activities. It also means that you stretch yourself. One of the great findings of the flow research is that to experience flow, you have to get out of your comfort zone and stretch yourself to a challenging level. I love that! Happy people are *alive* people. They get up every day and push themselves to be more than they were yesterday. This means that in the different contexts of your life, you push yourself. In your marriage or closest relationships, you take a step past where you have been before.

For example, you open up at a deeper level and risk sharing your fears or more vulnerable feelings. It means that in your job, you push yourself to accomplish things that you never have tried before, and as a result of that growth step, you get more invested and invigorated. You "wake up." It means that in areas of personal growth, you attempt things that stretch your skill levels. It may mean that you take some risks and learn some new hobbies or skills.

It is all about being alive at deep, invested levels. We can do some of the same activities over and over to the point where we are no longer awake when we do them. Flow, timelessness, happiness, and fulfillment all involve being wholeheartedly engaged, and getting there means we involve ourselves in activities that capture us. They grab our hearts and invite us to truly show up. Does mindless TV do that for you? Probably not. Instead, why not spend your time doing something that captivates your whole person. As Martin Seligman writes:

> Given all the benefits and the flow that the gratifications produce, it is very puzzling that we often choose pleasure (and worse, displeasure) over gratification. In the nightly choice between reading a good book and watching a sitcom on television, we often choose the latter—although surveys

show again and again that the average mood while watching sitcoms on television is mild depression. Habitually choosing the easy pleasures over the gratifications may have untoward consequences.[3]

So there are two lessons here. _First_, get fully involved in whatever you are doing, and find ways to make yourself more invested. _Second_, make sure you are choosing activities and ways to spend your time that can fully engage you. Pick worthwhile things to do, things that make time go away, as opposed to "passing the time." Let's unpack these two lessons.

FULL ENGAGEMENT AND WORTHWHILE ACTIVITIES

Exploring these lessons may take some soul searching in two different directions.

Be Fully Engaged

Maybe you are choosing worthwhile ways to spend your time but are not fully engaged. Your fears, conflicts, or worry may be getting in the way. If so, commit to "being there" when you are there. You may have to take some steps in those activities in a way that stretches you. But however you do it, if it is worth doing, it is worth doing with your whole heart.

The entire message of the Bible is that wholeheartedness is the only way to live:

> *You, my son Solomon,*
> *acknowledge the God of your father,*
> *and serve him with wholehearted devotion*
> *and with a willing mind,*
> *for the LORD searches every heart*
> *and understands every motive behind the thoughts.*[4]

God knows when our hearts are in something and when they are not. And, to be real about it, so does everyone else! Think about the people you know. Look at their lives. The ones who are truly happy are the wholehearted, engaged people. People who are happy in their marriage give all of themselves to the relationship. They are "in it." People with great kids and who love parenting are "fully in." The high performers in their work are 100 percent engaged. How frustrating it is to be on a work team with someone who is not. Who are the "in shape" and healthy people? Not the ones who work out halfheartedly twice a year. There is only one way to live life if you are going to be happy: totally in, totally engaged.

Otherwise, you really aren't living, as the flow and happiness research and the Bible show us.

THE LAW OF HAPPINESS

There is only one way to live life if you are going to be happy: totally in, totally engaged.

Choose Worthwhile Activities

As you move toward being fully engaged, you may have to ask yourself, *What have I been giving my time to?* If you are spending all your time in mind-numbing activities, it is time to stop those and "wake up." Pick some things to do that are worth your full engagement and will invite you to be there. You will be much more fully alive.

In my own work over the years, there have been seasons where I had been doing the same things for a long time and had gotten stuck on autopilot. I would feel myself becoming less alive. But at those junctures, as I would seek God for what was next, he brought opportunities to me that I had not expected and which were quite exciting. There was just one thing that all of them had in common: *I had never done them before, and they required me to stretch, risk, and grow.* And each time,

I can tell you, I was scared. I did not know if I could pull it off. But those activities also called for me to be fully awake. For many of them, I had to do a lot of research or get more training or seek out the wisdom of mentors and consultants. They made me grow.

I do a lot of public speaking nowadays, sometimes to arena-sized audiences or satellite downlink events with over a hundred thousand people. The first time I did one of those, I can assure you I was feeling the heat. But that anxiety was *nothing* compared to the first speaking event I did way back when I was just beginning to learn to speak in public. And there were only about forty people in the audience! I was petrified. Scared beyond belief. But God led me to stretch myself, and the natural result when we stretch is that we grow. Now a hundred thousand people seems a lot easier than that forty did in the beginning. I can actually enjoy the experience. But I also remember something else about each one of those windows of stretching times: *they were very happy times.* I was scared, as I said. But I was challenged and alive. And they were some of the best times of my life. They were times of *flow.*

Ask God what is next for you. It may be something new that stretches you into a flow experience. Or it may mean getting engaged in what is right before you. Perhaps you need to reorganize your job description or career so that you spend more time doing what you are best at and what engages you to the max. Research shows that businesses that use their people that way have the best performance. Work with your boss to maximize your gifts.

Either way, whether it is showing up more in what you are already doing, or doing some new tasks, do not let time just slowly go by. Make it go away, as you taste a bit of heaven by living a fully engaged life.

7

ℋ𝒶ppy People Connect

PATRICK HAD REACHED his career goals faster than most. Becoming the head of a significant company in his early thirties exceeded even his own expectations. His innovation was capturing the attention of his industry and that of the financial players. Investors were coming alongside him and throwing money at almost whatever he wanted to do next. He was riding high, seemingly having the Midas touch.

Behind the scenes, however, things were not all they seemed to be. While it was actually true that his performance was what it was and he was genuinely excited about it, that excitement gave way at times to another life. He had a "secret life" that no one knew about. Other than the numerous women with whom he was carrying on his affairs, he was also engaged in some other risky behaviors that were diametrically opposed to his calculated executive functioning. When flying across the country at times, he would stop off in Vegas, blow lots of money, and party in ways not becoming to a well-known CEO. If his board or the business journals could have seen him, they might not have recognized him at all.

Until they did. They recognized him because the women started to talk. Slowly, it all came tumbling down as a couple of the women decided they were tired of being in the shadows and came forward with some significant demands. They were not happy with having to be convenient to his whims, available on his schedule, and having to play second fiddle to the rest of his life, including his family. The image that he had built of the prudent corporate steward was blown.

Initially, he was devastated. He tried to do damage control and mount a defense, but with all the information surfacing, it was hopeless. He finally came clean with his board and other significant stakeholders, whom his behavior could have put in precarious positions. He confessed it all—even facts that had not come out—apologized, and was remorseful.

But besides that, he came clean *personally*. He told his board and those around him that he truly wanted to change his life and needed help to do it. His board asked me to be a coach through the process. Besides gaining a coaching relationship, he also entered therapy, and I encouraged him to join a leadership support group. He was, in my view, getting serious about his life.

What surfaced as we began to look at the whole picture was that he had always been a "star performer" and had pretty much always been under pressure to look good, make the grade, and carry the baton for whomever he was associated with. Growing up, he was the typical family "hero," the one who never needed anything from anyone else, always the strong one, and always the one who took care of others. What I zeroed in on was the total lack of support in his life and the degree of emotional isolation that he lived with. But when I mentioned it to him, he had no idea what I was talking about.

As we processed it, he came to understand that he trusted and depended on no one, and at a deep level, *no one was really that connected to him.* He had a lot of interaction with people but not from the parts of himself that needed it, such as his more vulnerable feelings of fear, aloneness, or hurt. He had always just covered those aspects of his life up with more "gold medals and trophy's." What he did not understand, though, was that this vacuum in his heart, this hunger for people to know him and his internal struggles, was what was fueling his out-of-control, risky, and indeed addictive behavior. He had to learn a new way of being. He had to learn how to talk to people about how he was feeling, even when he was not "winning." or "performing." He had to express his needs, hurts, and fears.

"So, what are you talking about when you say I need to be dependent on people?" he asked.

"I mean that when you are feeling crummy or afraid or just alone, I want you to call one of the people who have made themselves available to you and talk to him about it. And I want you to do that with your group and with your therapist as well."

"So I'm supposed to tell them what I have been going through?" he asked.

"Not exactly," I said. "Tell them *when you are going through it. Call them when you are feeling that way.*"

"You've got to be kidding," he said. "Call them and whine?"

"I wouldn't call it whining," I said. "I would call it being honest. It is, after all, a true part of you and your life. But since you have been denying it, your heart and soul is hungry for connection and comfort and has a life of its own, looking for what it needs. Until you begin to feed it real food, instead of sensual experiences, you will always be in trouble."

He got it and began doing what we'd discussed. He began

to go to his support groups, open up to friends, lean on them at times when he was hurting, and invite his wife into the shadow parts of his heart. His authenticity with all of this was a key reason that she decided to stick it out. As he remained real and genuine with her and others, he became a different person.

"I don't know how to describe this," he said. "But I feel alive for the first time in my life. I know I've had a lot of great experiences in my life, the highs of great successes, but this is different. The only word I can use is 'life.' It is as if 'life' is growing inside of me. I can feel it every day when I wake up. I just feel alive.

"The weird part of it is that I was, or possibly am, still close to losing everything I have, and yet I feel better than I have ever felt," he commented.

"How do you explain that?" I asked.

"The only thing I know to say is that for the first time in my life I feel like people love me . . . just me. I am for sure not performing well, so the fact that they are accepting me now in all this mess that I've created makes me feel like they really care. And that is the best feeling I have ever had. I feel like that word you said, 'connected' to them more than I ever have. I guess I always thought people liked me because I did a good job, but this is different."

He thought he was talking nonsense, as putting this into words made no sense to him. He just knew his experience. But it was not nonsense at all. It was the most foundational aspect of human life. It is called "bonding" or "connection," in the popular language. The New Testament says that our hearts are to be "knit together,"[1] to create a "bond of unity."[2] It is no Sunday-school jargon or psychobabble either. It is the most important aspect of human functioning: without bonding, we die. Period.

Even though Patrick had all the accomplishments and accolades that he thought would make him happy, God has not constructed us to be fueled by accomplishments, possessions, or trophies. He has constructed us to be fueled by love. And love only comes from being deeply connected to others.

THE LAW OF HAPPINESS

God has not constructed us to be fueled by accomplishments. He has constructed us to be fueled by love.

This example of God's ways is one of the most proven by research. We know more about the value of connection and the destructiveness of isolation than about most anything else. When people have strong support systems where they are processing their needs, feelings, fears, and so forth, they are:

- Physically healthier, with stronger immune systems, and less illness.
- Medically more likely to deal with their illnesses and treatment well.
- Emotionally healthier, with less stress, depression, and anxiety.
- More likely to reach their attempts to change their lives.
- More able to reach their goals.

And more. This entire book could be filled with the research findings regarding the power of relationships for our well-being. Everything we do and care about is affected by the quality, amount, and level of connection that we have in our lives, both on the positive as well as the negative side of life. Meaningful, deep connections with other people help you get to the good things that you desire, as well as help you overcome the negative patterns, behaviors, and syndromes that are hurting you.

THE POWER OF PEOPLE SUPPORT

Simple observation: have you ever noticed that people struggling with an addiction who make promise after promise to quit and never do finally get sober when, and only when, they join some kind of recovery program that has group support?

Have you ever known someone who has tried to lose weight year after year and has never been successful, and then upon joining a good program that has group support, he finally succeeded?

What about a person who has struggled with a difficult relationship because she was codependent or an enabler and year after year has found her life controlled by an irresponsible or abusive or addicted person, unable to get unstuck? And then, she joins a codependency group and finally finds the courage to not only set some boundaries but also get healthier herself?

Or on the positive side of life, have you ever noticed someone who wanted to reach some goals or develop a business and succeeded only after he got the kind of support and coaching he needed?

We've all seen turnarounds like these happen; the strategy resonates with common sense. But there is a reason it is so often successful: it is the way God designed life to work, and, in fact, it works no other way. Your brain, your heart, your soul, and your body respond to relationships with others. Relationships are where we get our fuel, our motivation, our sustaining power, and more. Your brain chemistry, for example, changes with support, as does your immune system.

One of my favorite studies is one in which researchers put monkeys in a high-stress situation and measure the stress hormones in the monkeys' brains. After the baseline measurement was made, scientists changed none of the stress (loud noises, lights, and so forth) and did only one thing differently: *they put another monkey in the cage.* When they measured the stress hormones again, these were reduced by about half. Just because the monkey had a buddy in there with him!

Remember the happiness formula that we looked at earlier, how almost half of your happiness comes from matters that you can control (10 percent circumstances, 50 percent natural wiring, and 40 percent practices that we control)? Remember, no difference in circumstances or in the monkey's genes were introduced. The difference in stress level occurred because of the other 40 percent in a person's life, the part he or she can control: *whether or not you are alone in a stressful world.* And just like the monkey's stress level was cut in half, we know from research that the same kind of relief can be yours as well. Get some other monkeys in the cage of life with you.

It is why the Bible tells us to weep with those who weep, to encourage one another when needed, to strengthen one another where we are weak. It is the reason military fighters who parachute into war zones immediately try to ascertain, "Where is my buddy?" We need one another. It is God's design.

I did a consulting project once where we were strategizing to up the sales of a national insurance company. Before designing the program, we researched various regions' baseline sales numbers and practices. In comparing them, we uncovered a significant finding that got everyone's attention: the regions that had structured team meetings with support, encouragement, motivation, brainstorming, and celebration far surpassed the others in sales and satisfaction. From there, we were able to design a program that helped the other ones do similar activities, and they greatly improved.

Why? God made us that way. He made our brains to chemically respond in a positive way to support from others and to respond negatively when we don't have it. He made our hearts and souls to do the same. Beyond that, our bodies also thrive when we are connected. Our health is better, our hearts are stronger, and our immune systems fight off sickness and stress much more effectively. In short, we need one another.

THE LAW OF HAPPINESS

God made our brains to chemically respond in a positive way to support from one another and to respond negatively when we don't have it.

HAVE IT YOUR WAY

One thing I learned from my mom when I would call her for one of her famous Southern recipes: there was not just one way to do something. If you don't have oil, just use a little butter. If you are out of flour, a little Bisquick will do. I can still hear her say, *"Oh, that's okay. Just throw a little of _____ in there. It will be fine."* She seemed to have a work-around for anything. As a psychologist, I have found this to be similar when it comes to connectedness. There is no one right way to do it, but what is important is that you *are* doing it.

You can join a support group or a prayer group. You could see a counselor or therapist or hire a life coach. Recovery groups are everywhere, as are neighborhood Bible studies organized by many churches. Or you could find a few like-minded friends who want to improve their lives and form your own group where you support one another. I talked to one group of three women who were all going through career and life changes who covenanted together to get on a conference call every morning at seven o'clock and go over their goals for the day. They said that in six months each of their lives had drastically changed. The structured support did it for them.

On the informal side, make sure that you and your friends get together and stay current with one another, on a soul level. Not that you can trust all of your friends with all your secrets, but the trustworthy friends are the ones you should be leaning on. If you follow this advice, you will be happier and probably live longer.

There is not just one way to stay connected. My advice is this: if you can do it on your own informally and it is meeting your needs, great. Keep it up. But, if informally and on your own is not working, then by all means initiate a process that is structured and more formal, such as joining an already-existing group or seeing a counselor. The key is adding one more level of structure past what is not currently working. Just remember: you were created by God to be plugged in to other people. He made you that way. So go out and follow his design; I promise you will do better.

8

ℋappy People Don't Compare Themselves

IN THE PARABLE of the talents, Jesus tells a story about a property owner and three of his servants. One of them was given five talents of money, another two, and the third was given one. The property owner went on a journey while they used their talents, and when he returned, he counted up the results. The one who had been given five talents had earned five more; the one who had two, earned two more; and the one who had started out with one was so afraid of losing it that he buried it and got no return at all.

The master, upon his accounting, was pleased with the first two. He said to both of them, "Well done, good and faithful servant!" for they had taken the talents they had been given, put them to use, and multiplied them. But the one who had done nothing with his talents got a stern rebuke for not even trying.

Most times, when we hear this parable, the focus of the lesson is on the third man's refusal to use what he had been given. So we are warned not to do the same, but to be like the first two and use our talents and abilities to do the best we can.

That is a great lesson, and in chapter 5 we saw how investing ourselves in worthwhile goals does indeed contribute to our happiness. But here I would like to focus on another important lesson that this parable reveals, one that research confirms and your own experience in life will confirm. The lesson is this: *we are not meant to compare ourselves to other people. God doesn't, and we shouldn't either.*

Yet many two-talent people feel something different from "Well done, good and faithful servant!" Instead of feeling like, "Life's good! I am grateful for the talents God gave me, I have worked hard, and look what happened! I did a good job. I have accomplished some worthwhile goals!" their perspective goes something like this: "What a loser I am. I was only given two talents, and with those two, I've produced only two more. I now only have four. Look at Rich down the street.

He has *five*. He is so much better than me. I am always doing less than he does. I bet he takes his five and gets five more. Then I will be an even bigger loser."

But in the parable Jesus says nothing of the sort. He in no way compares any one of them to the others. He only compares them to their own diligence in using what has been given them and making the best of it. He grades them against themselves and their own efforts.

Listen to the way the Bible describes this truth in another place:

> Each one should test his own actions.
> Then he can take pride in himself,
> without comparing himself to somebody else,
> for each one should carry his own load.[1]

What always matters is what you are doing with your own life. Comparisons with other people have nothing to do with reality. God has made you unique, with your own gifts and abilities, talents and horsepower, and to compare yourself with anyone else is like comparing apples and oranges. And research shows that doing so is a real mood buster. As one of the leading happiness researches, Dr. Sonja Lyubomirsky, says, "My students and I have conducted many more studies showing essentially the same result: *that the happier the person, the less attention she pays to how others around her are doing.*"[2] In fact, speaking of that research, Dr. Lyubomirsky says that when they initially asked happy people about comparing them-selves to others, "The happy folks didn't know what we were talking about!"[3]

THE LAW OF HAPPINESS

God has made you unique, with your own gifts and abilities, talents and horsepower. To compare yourself with anyone else is like comparing apples and oranges.

Kyle, an M.D. who had overcome and accomplished much in his life, was telling me one day how disappointed he was at this point in his career. He was in a thriving practice, but for him, that didn't mean anything.

"I am such a loser and underachiever," he said. "I should be way further along than I am now."

"In what way?" I asked. I thought he was doing exception-ally well.

"Well, look at Miller," he said, referring to a friend of his who was also a physician. "He has become a leader in our specialty through his publishing, sits on all the review boards, heads a department at our medical school, speaks all over the place, and consults with drug companies. I am not doing any of that."

You could feel the downer of his mood in the room as he was talking about his friend.

I asked him, "How many times did your father tell you that you were a loser, and how many times did your mother stand in the way of everything you tried to do? And how many severe depressions, one with a hospitalization, did you have to overcome to make it through medical school and residency? And how many tens of thousands of dollars of loans did you repay by moonlighting, holding down three jobs? Did you put all of that into the equation?"

Despite all of those life challenges, through faith and perseverance he was a success. I thought it was incredible that he had even lasted. Yet, the doctor to whom he was comparing himself had come from a stable background and had never been depressed a day in his life. Not that he had not worked hard; he had—but he had not begun so far behind the starting line as Kyle had. To me, Kyle's accomplishments were *far* greater than Dr. Miller's, and I told him so. If he'd had the beginning that his friend had, there is no telling what he would have accomplished. But he hadn't, and that was just reality.

Instantly, as I pointed this out, you could see him get into another compartment in his head. His mood changed. He said, "Wow, I never thought about it that way. I guess I am not evaluating the whole picture." From there he began the process of just looking at his own work and life, figuring out what he wanted to do and accomplish, without comparing that to anyone else. Fulfillment, as well as even greater performance, followed. And, interestingly enough, when he got in touch with what he really wanted to pursue in his field, it had nothing at all to do with the things that Miller had chosen. Kyle was much more interested in pioneering new treatments. Less notoriety, more lab time, and more happiness than being in front of a podium.

The truth is that even if you could match Miller's and Kyle's backgrounds and experiences, the comparison would still not be a good one. The reason is because they would not have the same genes, brain chemistry, hormone levels, talents and gifts, temperament, or personality. It just never works to compare people. Even siblings do not come from the same background. They come from totally different families, always. One has a mom, a dad, and a little brother or sister. And the other one has a mom, a dad, and a big brother or sister. Totally different families, even if other factors were the same. Plus, they each have a totally different genetic makeup. So comparisons never work. God knows this and warns us against it.

MEN'S VIEW OF WOMEN

So many women feel insecure about their bodies, their clothes, their hair, their homes, and everything else, because they compare themselves to women on television and in magazines, to celebrities, and with other data that our media-obsessed culture bombards them with. They are always reading the latest about what is sexy, beautiful, or stylish, and then they feel they are worthless because they do not look like the latest waif on the cover of some magazine. They cannot even enjoy themselves as they are always second-guessing their style or status in relation to others'.

Yet men do not look at them that way. A woman's attractiveness to a man has little to do with how much she looks like the magazine models. It has much more to do with her personhood, energy, and personality. It has to do with how much she is being "her" and not someone else. Women who are comfortable with themselves are way more attractive to men than the ones who are trying to be like someone in a magazine.

WOMEN'S VIEW OF MEN

The same thing is true about men. They often think that women care about how much money they make, their status, or other symbols of success. While most women do want a man who actually has a job and provides, the good women do not care much about the external symbols of power. They care much more about the personal and interpersonal strength that a man brings to their relationship. If he is confident, pursues her without fear, takes initiative in taking care of her needs, and is secure in himself, he will be very attractive to a woman. And, note to men: if she needs the biggest house on the block or the red Ferrari, he should run the other way.

THE LAW OF HAPPINESS

While most women do want a man who actually has a job
and provides, the good women do not care much
about the external symbols of power.

People are happy and attractive when they are themselves. God created each of us to be only one person, and to judge ourselves in relation to ourselves and ourselves only. Here's what the apostle Paul says:

> *Pay careful attention to your*
> *own work, for then you will get*
> *the satisfaction of a job well done,*
> *and you won't need to*
> *compare yourself to anyone else.*[4]

There is nothing wrong with getting inspiration from other people. We should be inspired by the greats in many fields as they show us what can be accomplished when we fully engage in bringing our gifts to our work. But if you play golf and can only enjoy your day if you set a course record or are better than Phil Mickelson, then you are not going to have a happy day.

God's advice, as well as the research, is simply this: do not compare yourself to others. Take ownership for your own life, your own looks, your own talents, and your own genes, and use what God has given you to the fullest. If you do, you will be the best you and the happiest you.

9

HAPPY PEOPLE THINK WELL

MARY HAD WANTED to be dating for a while, but it wasn't happening for her. She was an intelligent, fun, and interesting person, so there seemed no good reason for her lack of dates other than her strategy. Her "traffic patterns," as I call them, never placed her in situations where she met many single men. She worked in a small law office, went home at night, ran errands, went to the beach and hung out with a few friends on Saturdays, attended church on Sundays, and that was it. So, from my perspective, when you see basically the same people over and over, even at church, you are not really shopping. I had to get her "out there."

With much reluctance, she joined a dating service. I was so excited for her as she was finally taking control of this part of her life. She filled out her profile, and it was not long before she got an invite. And to her surprise, when she went on the date, she liked him! "I actually had a great time," she said, with a hint of optimism for the first time in a long time. I was happy for her.

I saw her a couple of weeks later and asked how it was going. I could tell she was not doing well, as her expression was lacking life. I could feel it.

"Not that great," she said.

"Dating?" I asked.

"Yeah," she responded.

"What happened?" I asked her.

"That guy I liked? He never called back. I told you this wouldn't work and that no one I like is going to want me," she said.

What she told me next made my heart sink: "I dropped my membership in the dating service. This is not going to work, and I don't want to go through the pain."

The next week, I ran into another friend who had read my book *How to Get a Date Worth Keeping* and was working the program outlined there. At thirty-nine, she had been convinced that it was over for her and had basically given up on dating. But I encouraged her to begin to work on it, and she had joined a few services as well. I asked her how it was going.

"Amazing!" she said. "I have found the greatest guy."

"Really? That's wonderful!" I said. "Tell me about it."

"I found him on that dating site you told me to join," she bubbled.

"Very cool," I said. "How'd it go?"

"Well, it did not start too well," she recounted. "But after the first few rejections, I just kept going, and then I met Jon."

"First few rejections?" I asked.

"Yeah, but you know how that is," she said. "You can't take it personally, and you just have to keep on going, thinking, *He is out there somewhere, I just have to find him.* And I did."

She went on the tell me the story, and it was great to hear how someone who had been stuck for so long was now moving and successful in an area of life that had been disappointing for her. The kicker? They got married later that year and just had their first child. Very happy.

The lesson in these two stories is one of the most profound in all of life. Here it is: they had the same experience, but one called it quits and the other reached her goal. The difference? *They thought very differently.* One of them, upon one rejection, began to think negatively about herself, about dating, and about the future. The other, even after several rejections, thought positively about the process, did not take it personally, and believed in the future. The result was that her thinking produced the reality she had been longing for, while the other woman's thinking produced the reality she had feared.

This is more than the old "self-fulfilling prophecy." It is the design of God. God has wired us to negotiate life based on our thinking patterns. It is a little like the navigational system in your car or handheld GPS device. When you are wondering what to do next, the software inside tells you exactly what to do. But what if the software was written with bad code? When you were ready to go somewhere, what if it said things like "Forget it, put the car in reverse. You will never get there. It is too hard. There is too much traffic. You can't drive anyway, and the people there won't like you when you arrive. Park your car right now before you have a wreck." Probably wouldn't make for a nice trip, even if you tried.

The reality is that every single day, happy people are thinking thoughts that help them to be happy, and unhappy people do the opposite. This is one of the most documented realities in all of psychological research: our thinking affects our moods, anxiety levels, performance, and well-being. Why? Because our thinking and belief systems were designed by God to do just that. They literally drive our lives in a way, just like the software drives a computer. That is why God said that he gave us his laws, "so that we might always prosper and be kept alive."[1] If the software that runs our lives is the very law of the one who designed it all, then we are running our lives in the way that works. Right from the mind of the designer.

THE LAW OF HAPPINESS

Every single day, happy people are thinking thoughts that help them to be happy, and unhappy people do the opposite.

That is what happened with the second woman in our illustration. She did not believe the lies going through the first woman's head, like, "You are not desirable. The future is hopeless. You can't make it through this." Instead, her mind had been programmed with God's truths such as, "You are my child and nothing can separate you from my love—even a rejection."[2] Or, "I can do all things through Him who gives me strength."[3] Or, "There is certainly a future hope for you."[4] Her software told her to keep going and God would be with her.

She had spent a lot of time working on the belief systems that guided her life and thinking. The fruit of her efforts was that individual events did not have power over her, but she had power over them. The power of your thinking is more powerful than anything that can happen to you. Successful and happy people are not overcome by their circumstances, losses, setbacks, or other events. Instead, they overcome them by thinking in the ways that God has told us to think—ways that breed hope, faith, and love. The things the Bible promises us "will never disappoint."[5]

OBSERVE YOUR THOUGHTS

Research has shown that what the Bible says is exactly true. If you want to find God's desire for you, you have to have your thinking "transformed." Here is how the Bible says it:

> *Do not conform any longer to the pattern of this world,*
> *but be transformed by the renewing of your mind.*
> *Then you will be able to test and approve what God's will is—*
> *his good, pleasing and perfect will.*[6]

To have our thinking "transformed," we must first observe it and see where it is off, where it is subject to having been conformed "to the pattern of this world." This often negative and hurtful world can teach us to believe some of the things the first woman believed, such as "You are not desirable and no one will ever want you." Some significant relationships in her past had programmed her mind to think like that, and she needed to have those belief systems transformed in order to have all that God has designed for her. I have every confidence she can do that. But to do it, she must become aware of the truth about those thoughts, that they are lies and have come from this world and are not the "ways of God." The Bible puts it like this:

> We use our powerful God-tools for smashing
> warped philosophies, tearing down barriers
> erected against the truth of God,
> fitting every loose thought and emotion and impulse
> into the structure of life shaped by Christ.[7]

It sometimes takes work to get our thoughts in line with the way God tells us to think and believe, but that is exactly what the verse tells us, to be "transformed by the renewing of your mind." But the work is worth it for sure.

What are some of the kinds of thinking that we need to transform? There is no shortage of crummy ways to think. But a few tips are helpful in terms of your happiness.

Avoid All-or-Nothing Thinking

Treat events as they are: single events. If you fail at something, so what? No one who has ever succeeded did not sometimes fail. The person just saw that failure as one event and tried again. Losers see the failure and think, *I fail at everything*. They burn the rice and say, "The whole dinner is ruined." They say things like, "I never do anything right," or, "I always get it wrong." All-or-nothing thinking and happiness rarely reside in the same head.

THE LAW OF HAPPINESS

*All-or-nothing thinking and happiness
rarely reside in the same head.*

And if you fall short of a moral standard, don't make yourself out to be "all bad." God says that there is not a righteous person who never sins.[8] When you make a mistake, accept God's forgiveness and move on.

Watch the Negative Thoughts

Negative thoughts have power. Everyone has them, but happy people let them fly by like a bird instead of catching them and inviting them to move into their heads and build nests. Unhappy people attach to negative thoughts and treat them as if they are reality. They allow those thoughts to dictate their actions. But remember, they are only thoughts.

Do not grab them, attach yourself to them, or let them have any power. Just let them go by and do not think anything of them, as they are only thoughts. One of the most researched and proven techniques of changing moods is to dispute your negative thinking with the truth and with positive thoughts. One way to do this is to refute negative thinking with what God says. If a thought says you are a loser, dispute that with the truth of God's word: "I am not a loser. I am a child of God, loved by him, and promised by him to have a future and a hope."

Avoid Catastrophic Thinking

Catastrophic thinking is seeing something as horrible when it does not have to be seen that way: "If I don't get this job, my life will be ruined." "If he doesn't like me, I will never find anyone like him again." In reality, there are few catastrophes in the bigger picture of life, and even when we encounter them, by faith we can make it through. But most of the time, catastrophes are only catastrophes in our heads.

"If I fail at this, I will never be able to face my friends." "It will be awful if . . ." Really? Is it really that awful? Those kinds of extreme assessments of normal life occurrences make people unable to negotiate the ups and downs of life and remain happy. They make taking risks almost impossible as they tell themselves, *It would be horrible if this didn't work out.* Happy people see those occurrences as part of life and say, "Oh well, that was a bummer. Let's see what I can do now." They shake it off and move on.

Remember, while there are certainly terrible occurrences in life, in God's economy, there is always redemption and a future. Always. With him in your life, you do not have to fear whatever might or might not happen, as he will be with you to help you make it through and get to the other side.

Do Not Overgeneralize from One Instance to All

Sometimes people will take one bad occurrence and overgeneralize. For instance, if they have had a bad relationship, they can believe things like, "All men (or women) are like that," or,

"Every company is out to use you and doesn't care." When you do that, it closes you off from all the goodness God has for you. The Bible says that God has a "good and perfect gift" for you[9], but if you generalize from a few bad experiences or people, then you will not be open to all that he has for you and your life.

The same holds true about you and your own performance. Just because you have a few failures, do not generalize from there to all future performances. Tony Blair told me that when he first ran for office, only six people showed up at one of his first speeches, and it was a terrible performance. But he said that getting over failure was one of the most important lessons a leader could learn. If he had generalized from there, he never would have become prime minister.

See Both Sides

The reality is that every person experiences good and bad. God promises us that. Jesus said that in this world we would have problems,[10] so we shouldn't be surprised by them. But unhappy people tend to block out the positive of many situations and see only the negative—about themselves, about others, and about experiences.

Happy people do not allow the negative to ruin things for them. They see the cons of situations, but they are able to still love and value the positive aspects. They do not allow the imperfections to ruin things for them. Happy people are not perfectionists who cannot enjoy anything that is less than perfect. Happy people are the ones who are happy even when there are flaws, missteps, and mistakes. The party can still be a huge success even if the cake flopped. The school can still be wonderful for their children even if they don't like the teacher or the soccer coach. Do not let little things that will *always* be there ruin the experience for you.

THE LAW OF HAPPINESS

Happy people are the ones who are happy even when there are flaws, missteps, and mistakes.

GOD IS BIGGER THAN THE NEGATIVE

Remember, God has told us that we live in a world that will always have imperfections. But he is bigger than the negative and wants you to still enjoy all the good that is here. Grasp his hand and do what he does. He stays involved and is able to bring good out of everything, even the negative:

We know that in all things God works
for the good of those who love him,
who have been called according to his purpose.[11]

Watch your thinking, and don't allow the negative to get you down. If you do that, you will be a much happier person. Arm yourself with this promise: "I will not allow my thinking to conform me to this world, but I will be transformed by the renewing of my mind."[12] Take all your thoughts captive[13] and "think well."

10

Happy People Are Grateful

I WAS HAVING lunch with a friend that I hadn't seen in a while, just to catch up. I had heard he was changing jobs but didn't know much of what was going on, and I was curious to see what all was happening in his life. He was a top performer in the entertainment industry and had been the head of a big company. I wondered why he left such an amazing position to do something new. *The new job must be really interesting,* I thought.

What I found out, however, shocked me: he had been fired. I couldn't believe it, as he was loved by everyone in the industry and had gotten stellar results over the years. There was just no way he could have been fired, but he was.

"What happened?" I asked.

"There was a takeover, and the new CEO of the parent company came in and wanted to shuffle the deck chairs, making changes as they often do for whatever reasons. I think he thought that making a change in our company would look good to the stock market, like he was changing everything, so I got the boot," he explained.

"Amazing . . . how long had you been there?" I asked, knowing it was a long time but not being sure of the exact number of years.

"Twenty-one years," he said. "Started in the proverbial mailroom and worked my way up to my last position. I actually always thought I would spend my whole career there, but it didn't work out that way."

"So where did you land?" I asked.

"Nowhere, not yet, anyway," he answered. "Unemployed."

"What?" I asked. "How can that be? You are one of the rock stars."

"Yeah, I guess. But nothing has come along yet that is a good fit. Talking to a lot of people, but not sure what I am going to do," he went on.

I knew that after twenty plus years, getting fired and not immediately finding something new must take its toll. Not sure what the answer would be, I asked, "So . . . how are you doing?" In fact, in happiness research losing a job has been shown to be one of the biggest circumstantial hits on people's well-being.

"Quite interesting," he said. "I am doing great, surprisingly, even to myself."

"How do you mean?" I asked. I've seen a lot of people who lost jobs, and he looked like he was doing better than I would have expected. I could feel the sense of well-being in his spirit.

"Let me tell you a story," he said. "In this time while I was not working, one of the things I decided to do was train and enter a marathon. I have been wanting to do that for a long time. With my work, I never had the time to train and do it right, and so I figured this might be my only chance. So I did it.

"Last weekend, I was walking up to the start line, and all of a sudden, my eyes welled up with tears. I realized something . . . I am so fortunate!"

"How do you mean?"

"I started feeling so grateful for so many things, like being healthy enough to enter a race, to begin with. For my family and friends and for the work experiences that I got to have at the company for so long. And get this . . . I was even thankful that getting fired had given me the opportunity to finally enter a race! Weird. Is that a sick way to think, doctor?" he laughed. "Am I in denial?"

"No, you aren't," I said. "In fact, you are right in line with the way that it is supposed to work."

He asked what I meant, and I went on to tell him of all the research that has been done in the last decade and how one of the most powerful findings, proven over and over, is this: *grateful people are happy people.* People who are grateful and practice gratitude regularly have significantly different levels of happiness than those who don't. And it is one of the strongest messages that God tells us over and over: be thankful.

> *Give thanks in all circumstances,*
> *for this is God's will for you in Christ Jesus.[1]*

Continually, the Bible tells us to be thankful people and not hide our thanksgiving secretly in our hearts. We are to express it, to God and to others.

> *That my heart may sing to you and not be silent.*
> *O LORD my God, I will give you thanks forever.[2]*
>
> *I will give you thanks in the great assembly;*
> *among throngs of people I will praise you.[3]*

And the research agrees. When we are thankful, and also when we express it to others, we are happier. People who express gratitude are not only happier but have more energy and better outlooks on the future; they're even physically healthier, having fewer physical ailments than those who don't express gratitude. They have less emotional and psychological maladies as well. Also, they show more relational capacities and are less envious and less materialistic. Sounds like the kind of people you want to be around, huh?

The good news is that you can learn to express gratitude and have it play a bigger role in your life with positive results. Experiments and clinical experience have shown that when people are given structured gratitude exercises—like writing down things in life that they are grateful for, keeping a gratitude journal, or calling and visiting people to express gratitude to them—they become happier as they practice those activities.[4] It is just one more example of how following the law of God is the same as following the law of happiness. God has actually, literally, wired our brains and bodies to respond, come alive, and do better when we are practicing certain activities. When we give thanks, our chemistry changes in a positive way from when we are envious or resentful. So, like any parent, God tells us to do things that are good for us. It is a spiritual equivalent of "Eat your vegetables. They're good for you."

I actually do that as a parent—not just tell my little girls to eat vegetables, but tell them to be thankful. And I do it as a psychologist-parent for technical reasons. Every night, when I say prayers with them at bedtime, much of the prayer is centered on giving thanks for various elements of that day or for their lives. My purpose is that they develop thankful hearts and minds, as I know they will be much better and happier people if they do. I want it to be a regular way of thinking for them. It's my job as a parent, and I think that's why God tells his children to do the same. He certainly enjoys hearing that we are thankful to him for all he does for us, I am sure. But at the same time, because he loves us, he also wants us to be as healthy and happy as possible, and telling us to be thankful instead of resentful and envious is part of the guidance of God as Father.

In All Circumstances

If you reread the first verse in the series of verses above, you'll notice that it doesn't just tell us to give thanks. It tells us to give thanks "in all circumstances." This is also significant from a scientific point of view.

First of all, it lines up with the findings of research that we have pointed out previously: only 10 percent of our happiness comes from our circumstances. So no matter what circumstances we find ourselves in, we need to be practicing gratitude to fill in the gap. Even if things are good, we can be vulnerable to unhappiness. This is one reason why you can find unhappy people in the best of circumstances. Their internal world is not in good shape, even though they might find themselves in a "good life." Gratitude can help shift that internal world in the right direction.

Second, it keeps us from "splitting." Splitting is a psychological mechanism that happens when we get into patterns of thinking that make the world, ourselves, or others into "all good" or "all bad." When circumstances deal us a bad card and we experience a disappointment or misfortune, giving thanks can stabilize our mood and sense of well-being. It can keep us from taking that experience and making it the "whole picture," thus seeing life as "bad." My friend who got fired is a great example of this. He is unemployed and doing well.

I saw many examples of this in the year following the Wall Street crash of 2008 and 2009. Working as a leadership consultant with many companies that were drastically affected by the economic downturn, I encountered some people who were totally devastated by the circumstances and some who were actually thriving. I remember one in particular who made the transition from devastated to thriving as a result of practicing gratitude.

He was in sales, and things were really bad in his industry. But when I went into the company to study performance and find ways to help them increase sales, he stood out as having one of his best years ever, even in the downturn. I asked him how he was doing it.

What he told me was that he was in misery and almost in the "fetal position" in the beginning months of the crash. He was not performing well at all, just coming to work and "staring at my computer screen," as he put it. Paralyzed.

But then he said he read somewhere that gratitude would be a good strategy. As he told it, "So I got a book and put pictures in it of the people in my life that I am most grateful for. And I made a list of all the things I am thankful for and wrote that in the book as well. Every day, throughout the day, I open the book and just meditate on the people and the blessings that I have.

"Then, on my drive home before I cross the bridge to the freeway, I stop the car and just get in my thankful mind-set. It helps me leave it all behind and it changes me. What I found was that I truly am fortunate and I truly am thankful. When I got in that mind-set, I regained my energy and my drive. My brain started working again. I got out and visited customers and made some deals happen and found some new ones as well. It all turned around, and in the midst of all the turmoil, I had the best year I ever had," he said.

I was reminded of that verse again: in all circumstances, give thanks. Good advice from God. When our splitting is overcome, we stay engaged and perform better. But not only that—we also feel better. We focus on what is good and don't let the bad overtake us. The old saying, "Well, it could be worse. At least . . ." is scientifically good medicine—for your mind and your body.

Third, it solidifies your character into being the kind of person who is going to be happy later, no matter what happens in your circumstances. Remember, only 10 percent is related to what is going on around you. The rest has to do with who you are and what you do. So life is always going to go up and down, and you can't depend on circumstances for your happiness. Your relationship with God, your relationships with others, and your life practices are going to be the fuel for how you feel, not what is going on around you.

In the economic downturn of recent years, it is sad to see this truth lived out. Some people, so devastated by the events, have totally unplugged. But thankfully, others are thriving, even if their wallets are not. They are standing on solid ground, practicing the "ways of God." To remind ourselves of what Jesus said,

> Everyone who hears these words of mine and puts them into practice is like a wise man who built his house on the rock. The rain came down, the streams rose, and the winds blew and beat against that house; yet it did not fall, because it had its foundation on the rock. But everyone who hears these words of mine and does not put them into practice is like a foolish man who built his house on sand. The rain came down, the streams rose, and the winds blew and beat against that house, and it fell with a great crash.[5]

No matter what is going on in our circumstances, his words about gratitude can make us stronger, even in the strongest storms. I have a friend who lost her husband under tragic circumstances. It was a totally devastating event for her and her three young children, and the going was very rough.

But in the aftermath, as she was recovering not long after his death, she was coping exceptionally well. I was talking to her and said I just couldn't imagine how she was able to function as well as she was, given what she had been through. She amazed me when she said, "It has been awful. I can't tell you how bad it has been. But I am so thankful for so many things. My family, friends, and church have been so helpful to me. They have been there and held me up through the whole time. I cannot imagine going through this without them. I feel so, so blessed."

Even in the midst of losing a husband, her grateful character was fueling her, enabling her to make it through the days. Along with the support she was getting (remember chapter 7), her sense of being blessed even in the midst of that circumstance was playing a big part in helping her make it through.

Life Is About Love, and So Is Gratitude

The other factor about gratitude is that it places us squarely in the center of the way life was designed: love and relationship. We were designed as relational beings, and we do best in every area of life when we are strongly "in relationship." Gratitude takes us there.

I was having dinner not long ago in Chicago with someone who is well-known in that area. When our bill came, the server told us, "It has been taken care of."

"By whom?" we asked. "Who paid our bill?"

"They wanted to remain anonymous. They just took care of it and said 'enjoy your dinner,'" he said.

"But . . . who? We would like to thank him or her. Who is it?" we pushed.

"Sorry," he said. "Can't say. Just enjoy!"

With that he left. And we did enjoy the dinner, even more than we already had, as now it was a gift. What an unexpected blessing. Except one thing . . . we were left hanging in a way. I felt a certain "but . . . but . . . who?" wanting to continue to come out of my heart. "Who did this for me? I want to thank them! Tell me!" It was like the full blessing of the gift could not be experienced without the missing piece of knowing who to thank. It left a happy but slightly incomplete, almost empty feeling.

I thought, *I wonder if this is what it is like to experience good things in life and not have a relationship with God.* You look at a sunset or appreciate a beautiful day or the face of a child, and that's it. What do you do with the part of you that feels grateful for such a wonderful moment? Who do you turn to? Who do you thank? Do you just feel "lucky"? I was thankful at that moment that God is there not only to give us gifts and blessings, but also for us to thank. It completes life and puts us in a relationship of love when we look to him and say, "Thank you."

In the same way, saying "thank you" to other people for whatever they have given you does the same thing. You have the gift, but to thank the giver completes the circle and the experience of the gift itself. Being able to say "thank you" to someone for what she has done for you, given to you, modeled for you, or just for who she is in your life is a wonderful gift in and of itself even beyond whatever she has given you. It will bless you to say "thanks" and leave you feeling happy and full. Being thankful and expressing thanks to someone puts you in the center of the way life was designed: in relationship. It bonds you to the person in a deeper way and cements the connection.

So do it. First, feel your feelings of gratitude. They will fill up your soul, create happy feelings, and increase your sense of well-being.

Second, put words to your gratitude. Write them down. Say them out loud. Keep a gratitude journal. Research has shown that having a gratitude journal in and of itself will improve your mood and help you feel less down. Happiness follows gratitude.

Third, tell them to God and other people. Tell them what you are thankful for from them and in life. Go visit a teacher from your youth and thank him for what he did in your life. Pick up the phone and call a friend and tell her how grateful you are for her. Tell your employees, co-workers, or boss. Make the practice of expressing gratitude something you consistently build into your life. The people you thank will be blessed and feel appreciated, and you will be better off too.

11

Happy People Have Boundaries

IT'S OFFICIAL. IF you don't allow people to control you, abuse you, or mistreat you, you will be happier. Research proves it, and the Bible tells us the same thing. But did we need scientists or God to tell us that? Well, maybe.

The reason I say this is that people who suffer mistreatment at the hands of others often don't realize they are *allowing* it to happen. They don't realize how much control they could have over their own happiness if they would stop allowing themselves to be mistreated and affected by another person's behavior. In short, they don't understand that they do not have good *boundaries.*

They think they are somehow doomed to be unhappy because of another person, or that they will be happy only if that other person changes in some way. The surprising truth, though, is quite the opposite. They will be happy not when the other person changes, but when they get in control of themselves.

"How do you deal with a controlling person?" a woman asked from the audience at a seminar I was conducting.

"What do you mean, 'controlling person'?" I asked.

"Oh, come on. You know . . . the kind who always has to have his way or is critical of everything I do and puts me down," she said. "That kind of person. What do you do with him."

"You convert him," I said.

"What? The person I am talking about has no interest in God," she said. "How would I convert him?"

"I didn't say convert him to God," I answered. "I meant convert him from being a controlling person to being a frustrated person."

"What do you mean?" she asked.

THE DIFFERENCE BETWEEN *CONTROLLING* AND *FRUSTRATED*

"Think about it. In reality, there is no such thing as a controlling person. You only describe this person as controlling because you give in to his having to do everything his way, or you give in to his criticism in some way. So when you give in, you feel controlled and you call him controlling.

"So my suggestion is that you turn him into a frustrated person instead of a controlling person by one simple step: *stop giving in.* If you don't give in to his demands or manipulation, he is no longer 'controlling' is he? He is *frustrated* instead. He is frustrated that you won't give in, but he no longer has control of anything at that point, does he? Just say no, and the problem will be solved," I said. "Then, empathize with him, and say, 'So sorry that it frustrates you that I won't do that for you. I understand.' It is nice to empathize with someone who is frustrated, but it's destructive to give in to someone who is trying to control you."

You could see the lights going on in her head. She had been so conditioned to doing whatever others wanted her to do or feeling that she had to put up with their put-downs or constant criticism that it never occurred to her how powerless those other people actually are, having no control over anything. She is the one who has control over herself and what she will or won't do, and what she will or won't put up with.

But let me utter some words of caution here: in some instances, you may actually be dealing with someone who is physically abusive, and if that is the case, or there is any possibility of that, then do not set direct limits on him if you will be in danger. Go to a shelter or get help from others. Your safety is your first concern.

Later the woman from the seminar contacted me and told me that she had "gotten it," and since putting better boundaries in place, her entire life had changed. Obviously, it did not happen as a result of one conversation at a seminar, as she had a lot of work to do. She even joined a group to help her and enlisted the aid of a good counselor. But what the seminar had done was wake her up out of the state of feeling powerless to another person's dysfunction.

This is one of the most powerful lessons to learn if you want to be happier. Psychologists have known for a long time that happy people have something called an "internal locus of control," meaning, they understand they are controlled by themselves and not by others or by their circumstances. In terms of boundaries, it means that you do not allow other people's control, manipulation, irresponsibility, or even abuse to be in charge of your life. Having boundaries means that you step up and set limits on what you will and will not allow in your life.

THE LAW OF HAPPINESS

Having boundaries means that you set limits on what you will and will not allow in your life.

The Bible has some things to say about setting up guards in our lives. "Above all else, guard your heart, for it is the wellspring of life," it says.[1] In another place it says: "In the paths of the wicked lie thorns and snares, but he who guards his soul stays far from them."[2]

Healthy boundaries guard your heart, your mind, your soul, and your energy.[3] When you set proper boundaries around your heart, you won't be tempted to do wrong to others and you won't become vulnerable to their wrongdoing against you. If you are not guarding yourself, then the predators and the happiness killers will invade your territory and certainly diminish your happiness, if not worse.

Take Control of Your Heart

When your heart is right, your sense of well-being, or happiness, will grow. So to increase your happiness, take a look at the ways you are or are not guarding your heart. Are you allowing someone to "steal your happiness"? Is there a person or persons who are able to manipulate you or "make you feel bad"? Is there someone who is actively hurting you in some way? If so, get back in control by not allowing that person or persons to affect you in hurtful ways. Note the way that David, in the Psalms, listed his boundaries, referring to the kinds of behavior he would not put up with:

> I will set before my eyes
>   no vile thing.
>   The deeds of faithless men I hate;
>   they will not cling to me.
> Men of perverse heart shall be far from me;
>   I will have nothing to do with evil.
> Whoever slanders his neighbor in secret,
>   him will I put to silence;
>   whoever has haughty eyes and a proud heart,
>   him will I not endure.
> My eyes will be on the faithful in the land,
>   that they may dwell with me;
>   he whose walk is blameless
>   will minister to me.
> No one who practices deceit
>   will dwell in my house;

no one who speaks falsely
will stand in my presence.
Every morning I will put to silence
all the wicked in the land;
I will cut off every evildoer
from the city of the LORD.[4]

Consider this question: look back at your life and ask yourself—how would my life have been different if I'd had the same boundaries as David? Here's how your list might look:

- I will not put "vile things" before my eyes.
- I will not trust faithless people.
- I will stay away from anyone who perverts anything good.
- I will avoid slanderers.
- I will not put up with people's arrogance or haughty criticism.
- I will not trust or be around anyone who lies.
- I will choose the faithful, good people to "dwell with" and be close to.
- I will make it a daily practice to set my boundaries against the wicked and all evildoers.

Most times when I ask people how their lives would have been different if they'd had the same boundaries as David, I can see by their expressions that there has been a lot of pain in their lives that could have been avoided with good boundaries.

PERFORMANCE REVIEWS

But you may be thinking, *It's not so simple to keep healthy boundaries in place. There are people in the world who would hurt us or put temptation before us, and we can't always recognize it at first.* True enough. But it's also true that people with good boundaries quickly address infractions and do not put up with repeated patterns of hurtful or irresponsible behavior. They nip the relationship or the behavior in the bud and deal with it, giving the person a choice: stop the behavior or face some form of consequence, for example, you can no longer be around him or her.

THE LAW OF HAPPINESS

People with good boundaries quickly address infractions and do not put up with repeated patterns of hurtful or irresponsible behavior.

Shelly was a talent manager in the entertainment business, overseeing the careers of film and television actors. She and I became acquainted after a media interview I did while she happened to be in the studio. After hearing my interview on boundaries, she walked up and introduced herself and asked if we could have lunch. We walked over to the cafeteria, sat down to eat, and she began to tell me about her work.

She loved it, she said, but she had some clients who made her life miserable. The few were wrecking her otherwise happy and meaningful career. They would get angry at her for their mistakes, be far more demanding than anyone would see as normal, and be irresponsible with their money—not following her advice—and then be upset at her when they found themselves in trouble. They were ruining what she loved about her career, she said.

"So fire them," I said.

"What? Fire my clients?" she asked.

"Sure, what's wrong with that? Not all of them, just the ones who are making life miserable for you. But you won't actually have to fire them. Just give them a performance review like you would in any other relationship," I said.

"A performance review?" she asked.

"Sure. Just tell them that you have certain expectations of your clients, as they do of you. You expect them to follow your instructions, to get the information to you that you need, and to treat you with respect. Then, tell them that they are not doing these things and that if you are going to continue to work together, they are going to have to do better. If they don't, then you don't want to continue being their manager," I explained.

"That's scary . . ." she said. "If they don't meet my expectations, then I will lose some clients, and I need their business."

"So now we get to the real problem," I said. "You are dependent on some not-so-good people. I think you had better address that problem first, and then you can do what you need to do."

About a year later, she called me and asked to join her for coffee. When we sat down, she was beaming. "I did it," she said. "I got rid of the bad ones, and I am loving my work. I could not be happier."

"That's great," I said. "How did you do it?"

"Well, first things first. I found some new clients and took on some part-time script-consulting work, so I knew I would have the income I needed to pay my expenses. Then I had those conversations we discussed. Some got mad and went away, and a few changed their behavior, but all in all, I now have clients with whom I love working, and I like my job again," she said. "In fact, it seems that I am attracting better clients now that I have changed."

"That usually is what happens," I said. "Change yourself and the world changes around you. Good job!"

THE LAW OF HAPPINESS

When you change yourself, the world around you usually changes as well.

I beamed. I love it when I see people finding one of the most important gifts that God gives us: freedom. Freedom from other people's wrecking their lives, or any other kind of freedom. God is into your not being oppressed. And he gives you the ability to develop self-control so that you can be free.

But to do so means that you get step one in place first, like she did. In the same way that an entertainment manager needs to get her financial needs met for security's sake, you have to make sure you get your security needs met also—especially, your emotional needs. Find a good support group or boundaries group or codependency group to support you and help you stand up to difficult situations. Remember, controlling people get frustrated if you attempt to convert them, so they may get angry at you. You will need the support of others if that is the case.

Either way, find support and protect your heart, mind, soul, strength, and body. God desires for you to be prudent, or wise, and not continue to walk into danger, emotional or otherwise—as is written about in Proverbs:

> *A prudent man sees danger and takes refuge,*
> *but the simple keep going and suffer for it.*[5]

In order to have the strength to do what you need to do, you must have the security of relationships with God and good people.

NAME YOUR BOUNDARIES

Sometimes, like David, it is good to think about and write down the boundaries that are important to you. Here are some to get you started:

- I will not allow myself to be yelled at or verbally abused. If that happens, I will distance myself from the relationship until the abuse stops.

- I will not allow myself to trust a liar or a cheat. The lying must stop before I trust the person again.
- I will not take responsibility for the irresponsible behavior of others. If they try to get me to do their work, I will tell them I care for them, but that it is their responsibility, not mine.
- I will not allow myself to be around substance abusers.
- I will not tolerate abuse of any kind.
- I will not allow myself to be constantly criticized or infected with toxic emotional treatment that damages me. I will address it and try to resolve it, but if the situation cannot be resolved, I will not expose myself to it.
- I will not allow someone to derail me from my path of growth or my relationship with God.

Of course, the above list looks only at staying free from other people's wrongs toward us, but we also need to keep ourselves away from people who would tempt us to do wrong. Everyone's list will be different, depending on where each one needs specific boundaries. The list above belonged to someone who had a history of putting up with some bad treatment in hurtful relationships. Yours may not be so serious but could have more to do with reaching your goals or building your life in a different direction. An example would be, "I will not allow my time to get sidetracked by too many people needing things from me. I will guard my time for this season to get _____ accomplished." Boundaries are important not only to protect you from evil, but to protect the good things you are trying to build.

THE LAW OF HAPPINESS

Boundaries not only protect you from evil, but protect the good things you are trying to build.

Another writing example from yours truly: When I am writing a book, I have to block out time and protect it, or I will never get it done. When a deadline approaches, it seems weird to say to someone, especially a friend, "I would love to have lunch with you. Can you call me in about four months?" Sometimes the person looks at me like I'm a bit nuts, but if I didn't do that during busy times, I would never get the book done.

Guard your dreams, your passions, your time, your energy, your heart, your mind, and your soul. You guard these treasures not because of selfishness—as boundaries are not meant to turn you into a self-centered person—but so you will have treasures to spend on serving in the ways that matter to the people you truly want to give to—including yourself. You can have some treasures for yourself and some for others too. If you have these kinds of boundaries, you will be guarding your happiness as well.

> Set a guard over my mouth, O LORD;
> keep watch over the door of my lips.[6]

12

*H*APPY PEOPLE FORGIVE

I HAVE TWO friends who don't know each other but might as well have been sisters, or at least cousins. What I mean is that Rachel and Susan grew up in very similar homes, both suffering terrible mistreatment, even abuse. How either of them is walking around today is a miracle to God's faithfulness in their lives. But there are some major differences between the two.

Rachel is difficult to get close to. She is suspicious and has a bit of cynicism about her that, although it's somewhat funny, it sometimes gets in the way of her ability to relate.

Susan is emotionally and relationally open, and if you are a good, trustworthy person, she is available to connect with. When you are with her, you sense that she is present.

Rachel has an edge. In working with her, people can at times find her abrasive.

Susan is no pushover, but she is clear, direct, and easy to work with.

Rachel has difficulty in many relationships, with a lot of conflict, especially when she is slighted in some way.

Susan has longstanding friends and good relationships with all of them.

Rachel clearly has issues with men. She is quick to find fault with them, and although she desires a relationship with a man, she is in her forties and has never married. She always finds something wrong with every man she dates.

Susan loves men, and has good men friends as well as a good, loving, honest, and responsible husband of twenty years.

Rachel is obsessed with justice. By that, I mean that anytime something goes wrong in any setting, formal or informal, she is relentless about "getting the bad guy and making him pay."

Susan also pursues justice, and I have seen her go out of her way—even endure pain—for the sake of others who have been hurt or mistreated in some way. But you never sense that she's waging a vendetta.

Rachel is estranged from her father and has a strained relationship with her mother.

Susan has enjoyed as positive a relationship with her aging parents as possible and has taken good care of them in their old age.

They are both smart and talented women. Overall, I like Susan a lot and enjoy being around her. Rachel I can take in doses; usually a few times a year is enough. And although both are gifted, Susan's life has worked out a lot better than Rachel's.

Susan is, overall, a happy person; I think most who know Rachel would say that Rachel is not.

I do not mean to judge either one, and I generally do not think it's helpful to make comparisons between people, for the reasons we saw in chapter 8. I do not know what it is like to be Rachel, nor all of what goes into making her like she is. I know Susan a lot better, and I have a better idea about what has made her succeed relationally and otherwise in her life. But without judging or comparing, I cannot deny that there is one very big difference between them: Susan forgives, and Rachel does not.

And as a psychologist, I believe that Rachel's and Susan's opposite attitudes on forgiving account for much of the difference between their lives. But further, I believe that attitudes on forgiving account for much of the difference in the lives of happy people versus unhappy people.

WHY FORGIVENESS MAKES A DIFFERENCE

The Bible and the research both position forgiveness as one of the most valuable gifts we can possess. Not only does receiving it yourself help you immensely, but you are helped by granting it to others, by being a forgiving person. The evidence affirms that when you forgive others, you are the biggest beneficiary. People who forgive have better psychological and physical well-being, greater marital satisfaction, and fewer mental and physical health problems. In fact, it has been measured that nonforgiveness increases one's heart rate and blood pressure. Think of the long-term effects of that! Heart-attack survivors who learn how to forgive have been shown to be less hostile and suffer less heart problems, for example.[1]

THE LAW OF HAPPINESS

The evidence affirms that when you forgive others, you are the biggest beneficiary.

People who forgive have a host of positive traits that benefit them in their ability to get along with others as well as their overall functioning in life. They have a better ability to move on with life after something goes wrong, and they don't dwell on getting even by persistent rumination.[2] They are just a whole lot better off. If you think about it, who wouldn't be better off if they were not walking around with a lot of resentment, toxic anger, or hatred, and a head full of negative thoughts over an event in the past or toward persons who hurt them?

Although there is a lot of research to validate the power of forgiveness, as a clinician, I would not have had to read about it to know its power. I have seen the power of forgiveness proven over and over in the lives of people I have worked with. The ones who are able to forgive are by far the healthiest and the least hampered by what they have suffered at the hands of others. They are much more able to be who they truly are and construct the lives they desire than the ones who are still holding on to whatever offenses have happened to them in the past. The reason for this gets to the very heart of the mechanics of forgiveness.

Forgiveness is defined as "canceling a debt." In other words, justice demands that if someone does something bad to you, *she owes you.* She should not have done whatever it was, and she must fix it or to make it right. And, of course, this is true. You can literally "hold it against her," meaning you have a valid claim against her in legal parlance. That is why you sometimes hear the Lord's Prayer recited as "forgive us our debts as we forgive our debtors." The word "forgiveness" itself comes from the idea of someone's "owing you." It is also why you hear financial people make statements like "they forgave the loan."

Therefore, to forgive someone means *they no longer owe you anything*, because you have let go of the offense. Just like a bank writes off a loan and lets it go, in forgiving someone, you let go of the offense. You take it off your books and return the ledger to a zero balance.

The significance of this relationally and emotionally is huge. It means you have let go of: (1) the need to get even with someone and all the negative emotions that go along with that, (2) the desire to hurt her or make her pay or feel bad, and (3) the demand that she make it right with you. It means, in short, that you are *free*. In fact, the main benefit of forgiveness is exactly that: *forgiveness gives you freedom from the one who hurt you.*

Think of Susan and Rachel. Susan was hurt significantly by her parents, especially her father. But since she has forgiven them and worked through the hurt, not holding on to the offense, she is free from their treatment, and it no longer defines who she is and how she has to be in life. *They no longer have the power to affect her.* She has been able to become the person she wants to be: loving, trusting, open, and free.

Rachel is still holding on to what her family, especially her father, did to her. She is still resentful and has a negative stance toward them. She still expends energy in talking about how bad they were. As a result, her orientation toward life is limited by what they did to her. She is angry at men, untrusting, and has all the other issues I listed. Why? Because she is carrying the past around with her, and it is affecting and infecting the present. *She is not yet free from her parents and what they did to her.*

Her resentment comes out in her being and personality. It gets directed at others, even if she cannot see it happening. As Jesus said, because she cannot see the log in her own eye, she cannot see other people clearly either. It skews her vision. She distorts who they are and then reacts to them. You have probably known someone like Rachel. Because of hurts she has suffered at the hands of one person, they hold it against all people who remind them of that person—whether those people are an entire race, a gender, a position (like authorities), a church, or whatever. Unforgiveness affects our ability to see and have real relationships with people because we are carrying past debts and injuries into the present. That explains why a person stuck in unforgiveness will sometimes treat a minor offense as if it were treason. This "treason" includes a lot of past sins attached to it from other situations.

Susan is the opposite. Having let go of any desire for revenge or the wish for her parents to make it right, her eyes are clear. She sees each new person for who he or she truly is and relates accordingly. And when she is hurt in the present, she works it out, forgives, and, if appropriate, moves on with that person with no poison getting in the way.

Emotionally, the problem with unforgiveness is that you are actively, consciously and unconsciously, generating negative feelings daily in your heart and soul by holding on to a past offense. The very stance of holding something against someone generates negative energy within you, which has real emotional and even physical consequences. The research proves it and reveals how many pains and struggles are associated with unforgiveness.

But forgiveness "breaks the chain." It cuts the cord between you and a past hurtful event. It allows your present and your future to truly be just what they are and not a carryover of bad events from the past that has the power to poison the good that you could be having today or tomorrow.

THE LAW OF HAPPINESS

Forgiveness "breaks the chain." It cuts the cord between you and a past hurtful event.

I recently sat down with a couple that a friend of mine wanted me to meet with because they were having difficulties. I was saddened by the wonderful potential picture in front of me that was anything but wonderful. They had great kids, great careers, good friends, and community. But constant conflict. The main reason? She was unforgiving, even of slight offenses. Every time I would try to get them to see how to connect with each other and build something, she would immediately bring up some failing of his or a way that he had disappointed her. It was relentless.

I don't know how they will do long-term, but I do know it will in large part depend on whether or not she learns this most important truth: life depends on our ability to forgive. If we are ever going to experience the good that God desires for us, we must let go of the "bad" and the sting that it carries. The truth is that we live in an imperfect world with imperfect people. Simple logic tells us that if we are going to have a good life and good relationships, we need to accept that we live in a world where bad things happen and everyone we love hurts us or disappoints us in some way. So to experience anything good with anyone, even the best of people, we have to forgive their imperfections, sins, and transgressions toward us. It is just reality.

As Woody Allen once said, "Cloquet hated reality but realized it was still the only place to get a good steak." We might hate this world where there are real people who hurt us. But it is the only world in which we can find the "good steak" of good relationships as well. To have them, we must forgive the "not so good."

NOT DENIAL AND NOT NECESSARILY RECONCILIATION

When talking about the necessity of forgiveness (yes, I did say necessity), two questions usually arise. The first is, "So, what are you saying, that I should just deny what they did?" Absolutely not! In fact, forgiveness demands the opposite. To forgive something, there has to be a "something." The debt has to exist. Forgiveness requires a transgression for it to even be an option. If you deny the offense, you can't forgive it. Let's talk about the difference between *forgiveness, reconciliation,* and *trust.*

Forgiveness

Many dysfunctional people are harboring unforgiveness, which is affecting their current relationships or performance, simply because they are still in denial about ways they were hurt. Simple example: someone who has never faced some issues about their parents and so continually has authority problems with every boss he or she ever had. Hmmmm . . . think *every* boss is that bad? Not likely. Their denial is spilling over into psychological transference.

To forgive requires that you name the offense, feel the feelings involved, talk about the pain and the anger, and then grieve it. It has to be embraced in order to be worked through. This does not mean railing on someone or going into rages. It means acknowledging how you feel and then working through it. We know clinically that rather than "getting the anger out," you must own it and work through the causes. In fact, if you don't do that, you will never get it out no matter how many times you try. Anger breeds anger; it doesn't resolve it. Haven't you ever known a perpetually angry person? Do you think that terrorists ever "get the anger out"? Obviously "getting it out" isn't all there is. It has to be resolved.

Similarly, forgiveness does not necessarily mean reconciliation or trusting the person again. Some people are not trustworthy, and some will not admit their wrongs. Forgiveness has to do with the past. Trust and reconciliation have to do with the future. Trust and reconciliation are different from each other, but both are separate from forgiveness. You can forgive anyone. But to trust someone requires that the person be trustworthy.

Reconciliation

You can forgive what someone has done to you, as forgiveness only takes one person: you. But reconciliation takes two. Reconciliation requires that the other person own what he has done, apologize, and have a desire to reconcile and have a relationship, whereby he stops doing whatever it was you needed to forgive. This is why forgiveness is a key to ongoing, long-term relationships, as it is a requirement for reconciliation. But forgiveness is not a guarantee of the other, because to reconcile, the other person has to get real about what he has done and make it right.

Trust

But trust is a different matter. You can forgive someone for the past, reconcile with them in the present, and still be guarded as to what you trust them with. The reason? Trust is earned. We entrust our hearts and possessions to those who prove themselves "trustworthy." For example, someone could reconcile in a relationship and agree to move forward but only grant more and more trust as the other person's behavior proves to be trustworthy. This occurs in marriage often if there has been infidelity. The victim forgives the wayward spouse for what has happened, and they reconcile to move forward in their relationship. But trust is earned as the one who caused the hurt proves himself or herself faithful and committed over time with new behavior. Sometimes, this time period occurs over a therapeutic separation, with the moving back in together being a fruit of the proven track record of the offender.

This forgiveness issue is no lame, mushy matter. It is not just being in denial and acting like bad offenses do not exist. It makes it possible for you to be free from the past but doesn't ask you to be stupid in the future. You can forgive abusive parents for the past but be guarded in how much you trust them in the present if they have not proven themselves to care about you.

THE FUEL FOR FORGIVENESS

Hurt is powerful. It takes the wind out of our sails and gives us less zest for life. In extreme cases, it can even take away our will to go on. So where does the power come from to forgive the kind of hurt that wounds us so deeply? Where do we get the ability to forgive? Simply stated, from being forgiven. We are able to forgive others because we have been forgiven, by God.

THE LAW OF HAPPINESS

We are able to forgive others
because we have been forgiven, by God.

We love because he first loved us.[3]

God's love fuels us to forgive. Especially because he forgives "all our transgressions."[4] To the extent that we experience truly being forgiven of "all," everything we have ever done or will do that falls short, we are able to forgive others. We are humbled by his love and could not hold things against other people since a perfect God does not hold anything against us. He is our fuel:

Be kind and compassionate to one another,
forgiving each other, just as in Christ God forgave you.[5]

So when you find yourself having difficulty forgiving someone, remind yourself of how God forgives you. It is the standard for all forgiveness, as Jesus told us:

If you do not forgive men their sins,
your Father will not forgive your sins.[6]

It is wrong to think that we can be forgiven and yet not grant forgiveness to others. That is not even just. The choice that God gives us is clear: Which system do you want to be on? Grace or justice? If you want grace for yourself, then you can't be on a justice system for others. If you want justice for them, you will get it for yourself as well, and that means you will have to pay for your sins just as you are demanding that they pay for their sins against you. I don't know about you, but I am choosing grace!

And as a psychologist, I can tell you that if we have an unforgiveness gun pointed at others, it sometimes turns around and points itself at us too. The two often go together. If we are critical and unforgiving of others, it makes it difficult to feel forgiven ourselves. So do yourself a favor and forgive. But remember that God's love fuels us to forgive others. Bask in how he accepts you, for this is the God of the Bible:

> Praise the LORD, O my soul,
> and forget not all his benefits—
> who forgives all your sins
> and heals all your diseases,
> who redeems your life from the pit
> and crowns you with love and compassion,
> who satisfies your desires with good things
> so that your youth is renewed like the eagle's.[7]

> Who is a God like you,
> who pardons sin and forgives the transgression
> of the remnant of his inheritance?
> You do not stay angry forever
> but delight to show mercy.[8]

That is the fuel, the engine of forgiveness: the love of God. If you do not know that love, just ask him for it right now. Jesus offers it to all of us, and He tells us that it is free for the asking. And if you have asked, meditate on it, think about it, feel it, savor it. It will help you to be a forgiving person. And if you are a forgiving person, you will be happier. The Bible promises it, and research proves it.

13

ℋappy People Have a Calling

ONE OF MY favorite stories is about something that happened to me many years ago in the span of about a week. I was talking to a man in the homebuilding business who was considering a "career change," as he put it. When I asked him why, he said something like this: "Building houses has no meaning. I want my work to mean something. I buy a piece of land, build a bunch of houses, turn around and sell them, make a pile of money, and go to the next deal. It just doesn't mean anything," he said. "I hate my work."

Not long after, I was talking to another homebuilder, and he said something quite different: "I love my work. If it weren't for my work, I don't know what I would do."

"Why's that?" I asked.

"It just gives me so much meaning," he said.

"Really?" I asked. "How?" My first thought was *I wish you would talk to this other guy,* but I refrained. Instead, I just listened and was amazed at the contrast.

"Well," he said, "it starts when I look at a piece of land from the helicopter. In my mind's eye, I see culs-de-sac with children playing and greenbelts with playgrounds where they are riding their bikes. Then, when we design the houses and I meet with the architects, I make sure that the homes are planned in a way where they have great spaces for people to be together, like 'Don't put the kitchen around the corner from the den!' I tell the architects. 'Everyone should be connected so whoever is cooking is right in the action!'

"Then I see the fireplace where the stockings will hang at Christmas, where the kids will be gathered, or the stairs where a teenage girl will one day walk down in her prom dress to meet her date. When I think about how we are creating communities and homes where people will build lives, families, and friendships . . . what could have more meaning than that?" he said.

"I totally get it," I said . . . and I think I hid the mist in my eyes pretty well. As he was describing the love in his heart that was being expressed through building homes, it was quite moving. And a part of me couldn't help but think of the meaning and purpose that the first man was missing out on, doing exactly the same work.

DISCOVERING YOUR SENSE OF *CALLING*

Researchers write that, when it comes to how people look at their work, there are three kinds of people: (1) those who see their work as a "job," with its main purpose being to provide a living; (2) those who see their work as a "career," with the purpose of advancement upward on a path; and (3) those who see their work as a "calling," with the higher purpose of contributing to a larger good and for the intrinsic benefit and experience of the work itself.[1]

Which do you think is the most fulfilling and adds to happiness? Obviously, a sense of calling, where your activities have meaning and intrinsic value and bring enjoyment. When your activities create a sense of flow, the happiness factor goes even higher. Just think about how fulfilling it is to do activities that are in your areas of strength and are intrinsically and extrinsically rewarding. But all of that brings up a question: Where does this sense of calling come from?

Knowing Who You Are as a Person

First and foremost, your sense of calling comes from who you are as a person. If you compare the two homebuilders above, they did the same activities and from the outside could look somewhat identical. But on the inside, it was a different story. One was a detached, nonrelational guy who was in the building business mainly for money, which by the way we have already seen will not make anyone happy. The other one was nothing like that at all. He was a very relational and loving guy who saw everything he did through the eyes of what it meant for the real people, families who would live in his homes. It was about creating places for people where love could grow.

If you are the kind of person who is motivated by transcendent values and care more about the real things in life, as opposed to the things that do not last, you are more likely to see whatever you do, vocationally or avocationally, as having value beyond its just being a "job." It will be about service in some way, because that is just who you are as a person.

Realizing Your Talents Are a Gift from God

Second, your sense of calling comes from realizing that your life and your talents are gifts from God.

It comes from an understanding that he has given you gifts to enjoy and be fulfilled by, but also to use those gifts to serve humanity and God's purposes. Here is one of the ways he says it:

> *He creates each of us by Christ Jesus to*
> *join him in the work he does,*
> *the good work he has gotten ready for us to do,*
> *work we had better be doing.[2]*

If you look at your abilities only in terms of what kind of paycheck they can get you or how they can advance you "up the ladder," then not only are you not going to be fulfilled, but you are missing the essence of the story of creation. God created all of us, not just those in "ministry," to do his work on the planet. Every time I hear people say to ministers something about "doing the Lord's work," I cringe a bit. I totally respect people who serve in full-time ministry, and certainly they sacrifice much for what they do—and we all benefit. But the truth is: *everyone* should see himself or herself as being "in the Lord's work."

God put people on the earth and gave them gifts. Gifts to build houses for his children to live in. Gifts to grow crops for us to eat, and gifts to create trucking businesses to drive those vegetables to the grocery store for us to buy. And gifts to make grocery stores function so we can have a place to go buy food. Not to mention the roads it takes to get there, the cars we have to ride in, and the trainer who taught the checkout person how to scan your purchases and receive your payment, and the banker who will handle the transaction from your credit card to pay the grocer. And don't forget the gifts it takes to be a banker or to make the light bulbs in the banker's office so she can keep track of all that money. What about the police who keep your money safe and keep you safe when you go to the ATM to get some of it? Certainly they are protecting God's children. I could go on, but you get the picture. We are all on a mission to make the world work and be a place where people live, thrive, and love.

When we understand that God has an earth to run and that he put us here to run it, we understand that we are all in "the Lord's work." When we do that, no matter what we are doing, it takes on much more significance. As the Bible tells us:

Whatever you do, work at it with all your heart,
as working for the Lord, not for men.[3]

When we realize that we are working for God, every task becomes significant and meaningful. We are stewards over his gifts, and we each have a calling.

THE LAW OF HAPPINESS

When we realize that we are working for God,
every task becomes significant and meaningful.

Martin Seligman tells the story about visiting his friend, who was in a coma, in the hospital. While there, he noticed an orderly who, after doing his duty removing the bed pan, moved to a different task. He began rearranging pictures on the wall, even replacing a calendar with a Monet print he had brought in a shopping bag. After watching him for a bit, Seligman asked what he was doing. The orderly replied, "My job? I'm an orderly on this floor," he answered. "But I bring in new prints and photos every week. You see, I'm responsible for the health of all these patients. Take Mr. Miller here. He hasn't woken up since they brought him in, but when he does, I aim to make sure he sees beautiful things right away."[4]

It is clear to anyone that the orderly was not just doing a job. He has a calling, and I would submit to you that he is doing God's work in a significant way. He is much more fulfilled than a lot of driven, seven-figure executives who hate what they do but are in pursuit of "happiness" by climbing the corporate ladder or filling their bank accounts.

Having a View Toward the People on the Other End

Third, our sense of calling comes from understanding that what we do is all about the people on the receiving end. We are all in the service business, no matter what we are doing. In the aftermath of the Wall Street meltdown of 2008–09, I worked with a lot of people from several companies in banking, insurance, real estate, and financial services. If you recall, those industries took a serious beating, and it was quite difficult for them. I felt compassion for anyone whose business it was to look out for other people's money, as everyone's investments were taking a beating. If you were in those industries, you were probably having a tough time.

But in talking to hundreds of people in that industry and speaking to thousands more and hearing their feedback, I heard one theme over and over. The ones who were doing well and thriving saw what they did as a mission and a service to their clients, rather than just being in the "market" or the investment industry. The ones who in the darkest days found meaning and motivation were the ones who saw themselves in the trenches with individuals and families who were worried about their retirement, their kids' college educations, their homes, or just their ability to pay the bills next month. Beyond simply being bankers, CPAs, or investment advisors, they saw themselves as counselors and social workers. They were in it to help their clients, help them weather the downturn, and stay afloat, offering them support, hope, and courage. In that kind of work, even if their own portfolios and income were way down, they found meaning and happiness. One of them said to me, "Every day, my work has meaning. I know I am making a difference in people's lives." To me, that is doing the Lord's work. That is a calling, even if you are selling stocks or managing IRAs or investment properties.

Owning the Gifts God Has Given You

Fourth, your sense of calling has to do with seeing the world as a place where God has given everyone talents and owning the ones he gave *you*. If you believe—like the Bible says and like the research reveals—that every person has talents and a set of strengths, then you are careful to find out what yours are and put them to use. If you think that you have God-given talents to do certain things, then life is about finding those passions and gifts and investing them in real ways to produce real fruit.

Once you find out what you are really good at, all of life changes as you come alive and get energized about using your talents and abilities. You will also get a sense that there is a purpose to it all, that God made you that way. I remember a new mother's saying to me, "I feel like I am doing what I was put on the earth to do." She knew that her gifts were in being a mother, and she could feel the big picture at work.

USING YOUR GIFTS IN SERVICE TO OTHERS

When we are talking about a calling, it is important to realize that our calling is more than what we do for a living. Our calling has to do with using our gifts and passions to do good. That may mean as a professional, or it may mean as a volunteer. When I was in college, I discovered that my leanings were in psychology, theology, and people-helping kinds of activities. I began volunteering with youth groups and foster kids. I got no pay, but I spent my time counseling and helping kids in all sorts of situations. I remember how alive I felt, and I now know that was because I had found my calling. I was doing what I was designed to do. Not for pay, but just because it fit. Later, when I got paid for it, it helped with the bills; but the enjoyment and fulfillment was the same as doing it for free.

THE LAW OF HAPPINESS

*Our calling has to do with using
our gifts and passions to do good.*

Now, even though I am a psychologist by profession, I still spend volunteer time working with people, and I frequently find myself jumping into various situations to see if anything I know or have studied might help. It is just who I am, professional or not. I guess if you are a singer, you sing for a check, but if you are driving in your car alone, you probably sing as well. It is just who you are. But if I am at a friend's house and the plumbing breaks, I will not have a clue nor the inclination to help. And my friend will be much better off if I don't even try, unless he wants a flood. We all have different gifts.

When people feel a calling, and sometimes more than one, they feel like there is something that they just do, and they can't not do it. It is just who they are. My parents were about helping people, with a heart for the poor. Although they were in business for many years, much of their spare time was spent delivering meals on wheels to shut-ins, tutoring poor children after school in reading, or working with the Salvation Army. Their calling was to help others, even if it wasn't their profession. Sometimes profession, or career, and calling are not the same. In the Bible, the apostle Paul received a calling to tell people about Jesus Christ. He wrote much of the New Testament. But he made his living as a tentmaker. It is not always about whether or not your job is your calling. But it is always about *whether or not you find a calling of some sort.*

My daughters just finished soccer season, and it was a blast for me to watch them play. But I go to the games to watch, not to coach. And there are two reasons I don't coach: First, I know nothing about soccer. Growing up in Mississippi was a football experience, but not of the European kind. I kind of missed out on soccer training. But the second reason is that they already had a *real* coach. For him, helping kids learn how to be athletes is a calling. You can tell when you watch him. He is as professional about it as if he were coaching experienced players in the professional leagues, not little girls who sometimes were not sure which direction to kick the ball. He is following his calling to help kids. And he does help them. My daughters love the game, the experience, and him. And they are growing as a result. I don't know what he does in his day job, but for him, I am sure that Saturdays are the big day of the week. He is fully engaged, and you can clearly see, very happy.

The Bible and the research both say this: get inside the treasure chest of your heart, and find what you care about. No matter what it is, it will involve bettering the world in some way and using your talents to do that. If you do, you will have taken responsibility for your own fun and will be happier as you do.

14

$\mathcal{H}$APPY PEOPLE HAVE FAITH

I HAVE FOND memories of my father, who passed away a couple of years ago at the ripe young age of ninety-four. He was older than most parents when I was born, and I reaped the benefits of something he learned about happiness in his early forties before they even had me. In fact, his optimistic approach to life was evident when I was old enough to figure out that I was probably a "midlife oops" and asked him one day, "Dad . . . I wasn't planned, was I?"

He looked at me and smiled, saying, "Let's just say we always tried to make the most out of our mistakes." I still laugh at that moment.

And that was not an isolated time of laughter with my dad. He laughed a lot. If you knew my father and were asked to describe him, you would probably use words that all are close to the word "happy." I have heard him remembered most often as "jolly and joyful, always laughing and making jokes." It was just the way he was.

But, as he told me, he wasn't always that way. While he was probably born with the 50 percent or so of "constitutional happiness" makeup that I described earlier, and while I'm sure his 10 percent circumstantial happiness fluctuated with challenges and successes like it does for the rest of us, at a certain point in his life he became intentional about the remaining 40 percent that I wrote about in chapter 3. That was, I believe, the key to his joyful spirit and also his longevity. Remember that 40 percent? The big and good news from the research on happiness is that while circumstances and genetics play their roles, *the rest of what goes into your happiness comes from things that are directly under your control: your behaviors, thoughts, and intentional practices in your life.* The things you do "on purpose." What you give your attention to and what you give your energy to have the power to make you happy. These are factors that you and only you control.

He took control of that 40 percent at a certain point in his life and, as he would tell it, that changed everything. He told me he made an intentional decision in his early forties that got rid of the stress, worry, and strain that almost killed him. He had started his own company, and it had grown to a size that was, at that time, getting the best of him. Expanding into new lines of business, managing a labor force, and running all the operations were becoming increasingly stressful. He was maxed out, and at that point he had not learned positive stress-management practices. Two of the biggest stressors of all were an extra eighty pounds and what he called "constant worry."

He and my mother were in the movie theater one afternoon when he collapsed. Unconscious and unable to respond or move, he was rushed to the hospital, where they began to run tests on him. The conclusion was that his heart was in severe trouble, and they told him he could have as little as six months to live. "Go home and get your affairs in order," was all they said.

At that point, he decided to go to a large teaching hospital in New Orleans, about two hundred miles away, to see if he could get a better diagnosis. What they told him was that he had had a "complete physical breakdown," due to stress, weight, blood pressure, and other factors but that his heart was fine. Their advice was a little different from "go home and die." Theirs was something like "go home and start enjoying life." In other words, he was working too hard and was too stressed; if he did not change, it would kill him. They told him to reduce the stress and get a hobby. As it turns out, that was the advice that would lead to his full recovery—losing eighty pounds, finding a new hobby that he loved dearly, living for another fifty plus, *happy* years, and, I would add, being a great father. The question is, "How did he do it?"

What he told me was that he figured out that it was all too big for him, and that he was worrying himself to death, literally. So he began a new, intentional practice. Every day, he told me, when the workday was over, he would say to God, "I turn it all over to you, God. It's all your problem now. I'll pick it up again tomorrow. Until then, it is in your hands." Then he would go home and obey his decision not to worry, but to trust God.

Then he would go home, sit in his favorite chair, pray, and read his Bible for a half hour or so. This practice would reinforce God's promises and help him experience God's comfort and peace, and, as he would say, "Take all of that worry and stress away." Then, guided by his faith, he also put into practice the other disciplines in this book. All of them were grounded in his steadfast love and trust in his heavenly father. I can remember at various times, growing up, when there was some dilemma, his saying to me, "I don't know how it will turn out or what to do. I just know that God does."

It would be in my early twenties that I learned that same

lesson upon hitting my own "bottom" in life. (See the first book in this series, *The Secret Things of God.*) I found out exactly the same thing: when life is too big and we don't have the answers, there is a God who does.

THE BENEFIT OF *RELATIONSHIP*

There is a "law" that governs whether or not God's existence makes a difference in our lives. God had always been there for my father, but it was not until my father fell in that theater that he learned how God's "being there" could become something more. And it was not until I hit bottom that I learned the "law" that makes all the difference in "God's being there," versus "God's being there for me." That "law" is what the Bible calls "faith."

THE LAW OF HAPPINESS

Until you have a relationship with God, there is no connection, and you don't experience the benefits of the relationship.

The way it works is that God can be there, but until you have a relationship with him, there is no connection, and you don't experience the benefits of the relationship. But when you do make a move to connect with him, what the Bible refers to as putting your "faith" in him, then many, many things begin to occur that can change your life, health, well-being, and happiness. And the research validates this over and over, showing that people who are involved in their faith are physically and emotionally the better for it. As happiness researcher Sonja Lyubomirsky puts it, religious people are "happier, healthier, and recover better after traumas than nonreligious people."[1] One example of dealing with trauma is an eighteen-month follow-up study of parents who had lost babies to sudden infant death syndrome. As a parent, I cannot imagine how devastating that would be. But in that study, the parents who attended regular church services and said that their faith was important to them were coping better, showing less depression, and had greater well-being than nonreligious parents.[2]

Numerous other studies have shown the positive relationship of faith to physical health and even longevity. One study showed how "dedicated members of churches had up to seven years greater life expectancy than people who were not members of churches."[3] Faith and seeing God as a partner in coping with life has been shown to help depression and lower suicide rates.[4] The list goes on, but the findings are pretty clear: we do well when we are involved in a life of faith.

INVOLVEMENT IS KEY

But involvement is the key. I do not mean doing a bunch of meaningless religious rituals, but an involvement from your heart. My dad did not see his daily practice of turning his stress over to God and reading his Bible as a religious ritual. He saw it more like breathing or eating. His heart was involved, as he was truly trusting God with his life.

UNDERSTANDING TRUST

Faith is just another word for trust (see *The Secret Things of God*). It means that we depend on God for a number of things that make life work better and, thereby, add to our happiness. As Jesus said, when we come to him, we can have life "more abundantly."[5] As Moses told us, when we follow God, it will be "for our good," as he put it.[6] The Hebrew word we translate as "good" or "prosper" actually means "good" in a very big sense. It means things like "best, bountiful, cheerful, at ease, merry, precious, and so forth." Those are all words that describe happiness and well-being.

But just like a lamp must be plugged into the power source if it is to give light, we must be plugged into God through exercising our faith in a trusting relationship—like my dad learned to do. He believed in God before he started trusting him. But until he began to daily depend upon God, he did not experience all that Moses had written about. Trust is more than mere belief.

THE LAW OF HAPPINESS

My dad believed in God before he started trusting him.

How do you do that? The amazing thing about faith is that it is so simple a child can do it, even an infant. David said that God taught him to trust him "at my mother's breast."[7] Just like a baby depends on a mother for love and security, we do the same thing with God. Talk to him; tell him that you want to know him better. When you have a struggle or experience stress, like my dad did, tell God and ask him to help you with it. Go through your day in a dialogue with God, trusting him for all that you don't understand.

If this is the first time you have ever considered a relationship with God, look at it the way Jesus described it when he said it is like being "born" again:

I tell you the truth,
no one can see the kingdom of God
unless he is born again.[8]

Your spiritual life has a beginning, and Jesus said it begins by believing that he is God, that he came to earth to show us what God is like, and to show us that if we will trust him, we will have forgiveness and the kind of well-being that the research describes. So begin with that simple step, and see for yourself that his words are true, that if you seek him, you will find him and a lot more.

A RELATIONSHIP BUILT ON TRUST

Here are some of the benefits that you will experience from a relationship with God that is built upon trust:

- His presence will be with you.
- He will show you things about yourself and how to do better.
- He will give you the abilities to do what you need to do.
- He will give you guidance when you need it and shepherd you through life.

- He will help you grow and get past your "issues."
- He will give you more self-control.
- He will counsel you when you need wisdom.
- He will teach you about life and reveal truth to you.
- He will lead you throughout your life and always show you the next step.
- He will give you steadfast love and forgiveness that never goes away.
- He will heal you.
- He will bring opportunities and open doors for you when you need them.
- He will help you be more loving, hopeful, confident, and courageous.
- He will develop your character.
- He will provide for your needs and take away your worry and anxiety.
- He will comfort you in pain and loss.
- He will put you with people who will love you.

I could go on and on with the spiritual benefits of a relationship with God. But you have probably heard other Christians talk about how Jesus has made a real and tangible difference in their lives. I am not talking about some of the religious weirdos out there, but real people you've known who will tell you that he is real and that life is different since they have been in that relationship. But, as I said before, you will only experience those benefits when you take that simple step of faith, look up to Jesus, and say, "I believe. I will trust you. Show me the next step."

THE ULTIMATE MEANING

Besides all the benefits of a relationship with God listed above, which we experience day to day, there is a larger one. It is the benefit of having a life of *meaning*. We can live day to day and feel good by exercising good happiness practices, and we can use our talents to pursue goals and accomplishments that are gratifying to us as well, but without a higher purpose and meaning, we still are not living our lives to the level God intended. As researcher Martin Seligman says,

> The pleasant life, I suggested, is wrapped up in the successful pursuit of the positive feelings, supplemented by the skills of amplifying these emotions. The good life, in contrast, is not about maximizing positive emotion, but is a life wrapped up in successfully using your signature strengths to obtain abundant and authentic gratification. The meaningful life has one additional feather: using your signature

strengths in the service of something larger than you are. To live all three lives is to lead a *full life*.[9]

Faith in God connects us to ultimate meaning. When we know him, we understand that all of life has meaning and that we are here for much larger purposes than what happens day to day. We are part of his story and his purposes—which are most likely outside and beyond our own. We also understand that our day-to-day lives mean more than we ever knew.

Meaning in Our Struggle

Even our struggles mean something. God tells us he can use our trials to make us better people, and that he can bring good out of the most horrific tragedies in our lives.

> *We know that in all things*
> *God works for the good of those who love him,*
> *who have been called according to his purpose.*[10]

With God, when life does not go the way we had planned it, we know he has a higher purpose. We know that when we lose, *all is not lost*. He is taking us somewhere, and tomorrow has a purpose that today is a part of. Nothing is meaningless, and that truth allows us to throw the best of ourselves into everything we do, no matter what the outcome might be. That is a full life, with full engagement, even during pain or struggle.

And in other times where it is difficult to find meaning in whatever is going on, remember that to live for Him always has meaning. Here is how Paul puts it:

> *Whatever you do, whether in word or deed,*
> *do it all in the name of the Lord Jesus,*
> *giving thanks to God the Father through him.*

> *Whatever you do, work at it with all your heart,*
> *as working for the Lord, not for men.*[11]

THE LAW OF HAPPINESS

God is taking us somewhere, and tomorrow has a purpose that today is a part of.

Meaning in Our Service

The tedious work you are bored with even has meaning, as you are serving humanity as part of God's purpose. The simple tasks you do to make your family function have meaning as you are his arms and hands taking care of them. And when you give your gifts and abilities to serve through altruism and volunteering for God's work, in whatever form, you are part of a meaningful tapestry of life. There is a reason why my daughter had that warm feeling in her heart when she shared with her little preschool friend. God wired her to feel that when she was being an instrument of his love to others.

Meaning in Sorrow

Death does not fit life. Nowhere do we feel the need for meaning as strongly as when we lose someone we love. Death makes no sense, and when it happens, especially unexpectedly or to a younger person, everything within us screams, *This is not right!* The reason our souls scream that is because it is true. God has told us that death was not supposed to be part of our experience. It only exists because in the beginning the human race rejected him.

But a relationship with God can bring meaning even when we experience death. He tells us that not only can we understand it, but we can go through it and still have hope and the understanding that his purposes are still at work. He promises us that he is still there, that he is bigger than death, and that even when we die, we will be taken to him and also be reunited with those who have gone before us to be with him.

When my parents died within a few months of each other, it was a huge loss, but there was no despair. It was sad, but it was also a celebration. Those who knew them celebrated the meaning of their lives, as both of them had lived full lives (as Seligman says), serving higher purposes than themselves. They had served God and people and had been involved in many charities and other activities of serving the community for decades. Their lives had *mattered*, and we celebrated them—not only with sadness, but also with joy and laughter.

But more than that, we also celebrated that their deaths were not meaningless. They were a beginning of their new lives, the ones we could see through the eyes of faith. We all could see them completely healed, with new bodies, in their new heavenly home, with God. And through faith, knowing they are alive and happy today brings meaning even to their deaths.

Having lost other family members and close friends, I can attest to how huge it is to know that death is not the end for those who have faith. To know that your loved ones are still alive, simply in a dimension we cannot see, is not only immensely comforting but brings meaning to what could be the ultimate meaninglessness. Without faith, we could feel that "life seems so meaningless" when someone dies. But when we understand that God is still there, beyond death, and that he has explained death to us, we can thrive even when death is a part of the bigger picture.

Faith in God gives us meaning when we are alive, when we struggle, when we lose someone we love, when we serve, and when we die. In short, God *is* the meaning of it all. And when we are connected to him, we find out why we are here and what it all means.

OPTIMISM GROUNDED IN FAITH

How happy are you if you look into the future and see nothing but bleakness and negativity? Not very. The power of optimism has been shown over and over to affect not only happiness but performance and well-being in life. Optimistic and hopeful people are happier and healthier, both mentally and physically. Even their immune systems work better.[12] We can say from the research that optimism will "immunize" both your body and your brain.

Focusing on positive thinking and working on changing

your thinking styles is important, as our chapter on thinking shows. But positive thinking grounded in faith is even stronger. When we are grounded in our relationship with God, we can face whatever happens with optimism. We know he will bring good out of it and that he will lead us through and out of whatever difficulty we are experiencing. He promises to do that.

Not only that, but so much of the unhappiness in our lives has to do with our own failings, personal issues, hang-ups, and the fear that we can't change. "Why can't I be different!" is often the cry of our souls when we fail or when we blow it in some way. Well, the certain answer of the Bible is that "you can!" God promises to make us different, as we ask him to change us. He promises to transform us over time and turn us into better, more mature people, and the Bible says he will complete that process:

> I am certain that God,
> who began the good work within you,
> will continue his work until it is finally finished
> on the day when Christ Jesus returns.[13]

No matter what your last failure was, if you ask God to change you into someone who will be different, he will.

God's promises to take care of our needs, to lead and guide us, to create a future and a hope for us, and to change us into who we need to be are grounds for the most optimistic and, therefore, healthiest and happiest lives possible. As the Bible says,

If God is for us, who can be against us?[14]

That is optimism indeed. So when life hits you hard, and if you have faith, you can look to the future with a hope that is real, because it is grounded in Someone much bigger than you.

FULL CIRCLE

I have reported research findings to you about faith and also some of what the Bible says. But I have to add one last piece, which is more personal. And to me, the most powerful.

I told you about how God became the anchor of my father's life at a time when he was sent home without a lot of hope. I can attest to the same reality as well. I wrote about my story extensively in the first book of this series, *The Secret Things of God*. I won't repeat it all here, but I did want to say this one thing about faith, hope, and optimism.

When I began my journey with God, I had little faith, no hope, and no optimism. It was at a time in my life when I had hit bottom. I had tried to make it all work and was failing—in my performance, my relationships, and my emotions. I did not know what I was going to do in life or how to make relationships work, and I was very depressed. Not exactly in the position to help anyone, much less engage in a career of helping others.

In that despair of unhappiness, I reached out to God. I asked Jesus, if he was real, to show himself to me, and I promised that if he would help me, I would do whatever he told me to do. The short version is "he did" and "I did." He showed up, and I just followed.

The result is that he did what I have told you in this chapter that he does. He led me, changed me, taught me, provided for me, and did everything else he promises. That is not psychological, scientific research or ancient writings. It is the truth of my experience. And now the journey has come full circle. The one who used to be in despair is now sharing hope. To me, that is a miracle and the point that I want to make: if Jesus were not real, I could not have made that circle. I would not know any more about happiness than I knew then, nor would I be in any position to help anyone else, much less be in a helping profession! If you had told me then that I would be doing what I do now and writing books about happiness and hope, I would have thought you were a lunatic. And for all realistic reasons, you would have been.

But faith goes beyond reason, to a reality we cannot see. It goes past the dysfunction and hopelessness we may be experiencing, like I was then, and sees *who and what we can one day be because of who God is.* As the Bible says, faith is the "evidence of things not seen."[15] Just because you can't see God doesn't mean he is not there. Did you listen to the radio today? Or use a microwave? Music and microwaves that you cannot see come through the air every day. And the invisible God does too. He sends both messages and power to us that change our lives, if we are tuned in. And all of it is "beyond reason" and beyond what you can see. But it is as real as anything you can touch or feel.

So I invite you in your quest for happiness to meet the designer of it all. God created life, and Jesus came to lead us into it as it was designed. All you have to do is, like my dad, take a moment to ask. He will be there if you do.

NOTES

1. The Science of Happiness

1. Sonja Lyubomirsky, *The How of Happiness* (New York: Penguin Books, 2007), 20, 21.
2. Alan Carr, *Positive Psychology: The Science of Happiness and Human Strengths* (New York: Routledge, 2004), 32.
3. Lyubomirsky, *How of Happiness*.
4. Ibid., 20–21.
5. Ibid., 20–23.

2. Happy People Are Givers

1. Shankar Vedantam, "If It Feels Good to Be Good, It Might Only Be Natural," *Washington Post*, May 28, 2007.
2. Elizabeth W. Dunn, Lara B. Aknin, and Michael I. Norton, "Spending Money on Others Promotes Happiness," *Science* 319, no. 5870 (2008): 1687–88.
3. Carolyn Schwartz and others, "Altruistic Social Interest Behaviors Are Associated with Better Mental Health," *Psychosomatic Medicine* 65 (2003): 778–85.

4. Leviticus 27:30.
5. Exodus 23:16.
6. See Luke 12:15.
7. 2 Corinthians 9:6–7.
8. Exodus 18:18.
9. Matthew 6:21.
10. Hebrews 10:24.
11. Luke 6:35.

3. HAPPY PEOPLE ARE NOT LAZY ABOUT HAPPINESS

1. Philippians 2:12–13.
2. Hebrews 6:12.

4. HAPPY PEOPLE DON'T WAIT FOR "SOMEDAY"

1. Matthew 6:34.
2. Sonja Lyubomirsky, *The How of Happiness* (New York: Penguin Books, 2007), 197.
3. Ephesians 5:15–16.
4. Ecclesiastes 3:22, 5:19, 11:8.
5. See Luke 12:15.
6. See Proverbs 5:18 MSG.

5. HAPPY PEOPLE PURSUE GOALS

1. Proverbs 13:12 NASB.
2. Sonja Lyubomirsky, *The How of Happiness* (New York: Penguin Books, 2007), 205 (emphasis added).

3. See Romans 12:1–8.
4. Ecclesiastes 4:9–12.

6. HAPPY PEOPLE FULLY ENGAGE

1. Colossians 3:23.
2. Mihaly Csikszentmihalyi, *Flow: The Psychology of Optimal Experience* (New York: HarperCollins e-books, 1990), 1098–1103.
3. Martin Seligman, *Authentic Happiness* (New York: Free Press, 2002), 117.
4. I Chronicles 28:9.

7. HAPPY PEOPLE CONNECT

1. Colossians 2:2 NASB.
2. Colossians 3:14 NASB.

8. HAPPY PEOPLE DON'T COMPARE THEMSELVES

1. Galatians 6:4–5.
2. Sonja Lyubomirsky, *The How of Happiness* (New York: Penguin Books, 2007), 119.
3. Lyubomirsky, *How of Happiness*, 117.
4. Galatians 6:4 NLT.

9. HAPPY PEOPLE THINK WELL

1. Deuteronomy 6:24.
2. See Romans 8:38–39.

3. See Philippians 4:13.
4. See Proverbs 24:14.
5. Romans 5:5 NCV.
6. Romans 12:3.
7. 2 Corinthians 10:5 MSG.
8. See Ecclesiastes 7:20.
9. James 1:17.
10. See John 16:33.
11. Romans 8:28.
12. See Romans 12:2.
13. See 2 Corinthians 10:5.

10. HAPPY PEOPLE ARE GRATEFUL

1. 1 Thessalonians 5:18.
2. Psalm 30:12.
3. Psalm 35:18.
4. Sonja Lyubomirsky, *The How of Happiness* (New York: Penguin Books, 2007), 90.
5. Matthew 7:24–27.

11. HAPPY PEOPLE HAVE BOUNDARIES

1. Proverbs 4:23.
2. Proverbs 22:5.
3. See Deuteronomy 6:4–6.
4. Psalm 101:3–8.
5. Proverbs 22:3.
6. Psalm 141:3.

12. HAPPY PEOPLE FORGIVE

1. Alan Carr, *Positive Psychology: The Science of Happiness and Human Strengths* (New York: Routledge, 2004), 256.
2. Sonja Lyubomirsky, *The How of Happiness* (New York: Penguin Books, 2007), 172.
3. I John 4:19.
4. Colossians 2:13 NASB.
5. Ephesians 4:32.
6. Matthew 6:15.
7. Psalm 103:2–5.
8. Micah 7:18.

13. HAPPY PEOPLE HAVE A CALLING

1. Robert N. Bellah, Richard Madsen, William M. Sullivan, Ann Swidler, and Steven M. Tipton, *Habits of the Heart: Individualism and Commitment in American Life* (New York: HarperCollins, 1986), 66.
2. Ephesians 2:10 MSG.
3. Colossians 3:23.
4. Martin Seligman, *Authentic Happiness* (New York: Free Press, 2002), 166–67.

14. HAPPY PEOPLE HAVE FAITH

1. Sonja Lyubomirsky, *The How of Happiness* (New York: Penguin Books, 2007), 228.
2. Ibid., 228.

3. Alan Carr, *Positive Psychology: The Science of Happiness and Human Strengths* (New York: Routledge, 2004), 222.

4. Kenneth Pargament, *The Psychology of Religion and Coping* (New York: Guilford, 1997).

5. John 10:10 NKJV.

6. Deuteronomy 6:24 NKJV.

7. Psalm 22:9.

8. John 3:3.

9. Martin Seligman, *Authentic Happiness* (New York: Free Press, 2002), 249.

10. Romans 8:28.

11. Colossians 3:17, 23.

12. Carr, *Positive Psychology*.

13. Philippians 1:6 NLT.

14. Romans 8:31.

15. Hebrews 11:1 NKJV.

HOW TO CONTACT DR. CLOUD

For speaking engagements, consulting, or media appearances, email Dr. Cloud at info@drcloud.com. Also join him on Facebook and Twitter at www.facebook.com/drhenrycloud and www.twitter.com/drhenrycloud.

the
LAW
of

Happiness

READING GROUP GUIDE

This reading group guide for **The Law of Happiness** includes an introduction, discussion questions, ideas for enhancing your book club, and a Q&A with author **Dr. Henry Cloud**. The suggested questions are intended to help your reading group find new and interesting angles and topics for your discussion. We hope that these ideas will enrich your conversation and increase your enjoyment of the book.

INTRODUCTION

Drawing from the latest scientific and psychological research on the quest for happiness, *The Law of Happiness* discusses how the spiritual truths of the Bible hold the secrets to the happiness we desire. As Dr. Henry Cloud unpacks these universal, eternal principles, he reveals that true happiness is not about circumstances, physical health, financial success, or even the people in our lives. In other words, it's not about the factors that are frequently beyond our control. Rather, happiness is found in choosing to become the kind of people God created us to be.

As he unveils the connection between science, faith, and real life, Dr. Cloud reveals that *happiness is not what happens to you; it is who you are.*

Dr. Cloud shows just how happiness is achieved as he sets readers on a pathway of spiritual transformation that connects them with the God of the universe. With these new tools, readers will discover that their relationships, their careers, and their inner selves are infused with the joy they've been seeking.

TOPICS AND QUESTIONS FOR DISCUSSION

1. Compare *The Law of Happiness* with *The Law of Attraction*. Which is more meaningful to you? Which has more potential to be effective in your own life?

2. Think about a time you thought something would provide the ultimate happiness, such as a new job title or a new car. How do you regard that thing today? Does it continue to impact your happiness scale?

3. Is there a what or a when that is holding you back from seeking true happiness? How can you overcome those obstacles? How can you be happy in the now?

4. Have you experienced wholeheartedness or flow? During what activity? What other activities do you think would be conducive to a flow state? What inhibits it? How can you be more engaged in your life?

5. What are your goals for this week? Month? Year? Are they stretch goals? Are they SMART goals?

6. Review the tips for happy thinking on pages 114–119. Which do you already incorporate in your life? Which might you need to work on? What do all these tips have in common?

7. Do one of the gratitude exercises mentioned on page 125, such as making a list of things you are grateful for, starting a gratitude journal, or creating a book with pictures and lists of things you're grateful for. Share with your book club.

8. Talk about or make a list of your boundaries, as the Psalmist David did (reference pages 140–141 for inspiration). Which boundaries do you need to keep in place permanently, and which can help you accomplish temporary goals? Where in your past might you have benefitted from having such boundaries in place? How can keeping these boundaries in place increase your happiness?

9. Is there anyone, including yourself, that you have been holding back on forgiving? Why? Talk about the difference between forgiveness, reconciliation, and trust.

10. Discuss the difference between belief and trust in regards to your faith. How is it possible to believe but not trust? Have you experienced this in your own life?

11. Dr. Cloud incorporates both Biblical and scientific support for his Laws of Happiness. How does each section of his research inform the other? Which did you find most compelling?

ENHANCE YOUR BOOK CLUB

1. Review the activities proven to increase happiness in Chapter 4, such as serving others, practicing gratitude, and stretching yourself. Make a plan to do at least one of these suggestions, alone or with your book group.

2. Try the exercise in Chapter 5—take a moment to consciously savor two pleasurable everyday experiences throughout your day. Write about how you experienced them, and share with your book group. How did taking a moment to appreciate the now improve your day?

3. Has your group read *The Secret Things of God*? If not, go back and read the first book in Dr. Cloud's series. How does it compare with *The Law of Happiness*? What other topics would you like to see him explore in this series?

What made you so interested in happiness research? Have you always considered yourself a happy person?

In the beginning, I was looking into the research because of my work as an executive and performance coach. And the further I got into the research, the more I got interested not just from that perspective, but also from the spiritual implications that the research had. For the most part, I have always considered myself a pretty happy person who understands existential despair.

How do you personally define happiness?

I think of it in terms of the Hebrew word *Shalom*, which means overall well-being. I also think of it as a by-product of the word *integrity*, which means to be integrated or whole. Integrity makes us have good relationships and be fruitful in our work, which all affects our sense of well-being.

How do you balance working toward goals that you know will make you happy with living in the moment?

Actually, the research has a lot to say about that, and while goal orientation itself is a key component of happiness, the paradox is that it's not the reaching of the goal but the daily engagement of being in the process of working on it. It is the journey, not the destination. But goal orientation is a very important aspect of happiness.

Why do you think *The Secret* is so popular? Why is there such an interest in obtaining happiness in the world today? Do you see something flawed in our society?

I think it's so popular because it claims to answer some of the questions or issues that we all care about most deeply: what's behind the universe and how do we get what we want and need in our lives? I don't think the interest in happiness is new for today. I think if you look at the literature throughout the ages the question of happiness has been there from the beginning. I don't think our society has cornered the market on flaws. When you study history you can see that the real problem always has to do with the flaws in human nature, and that always gets worse when any society or culture encourages our lower nature more than it does transcendent spiritual values.

In terms of happiness, how do Americans rate versus other countries?

There are a lot of studies out there, but a pretty good rating would say that we are not in the top ten or even the top twenty. One big study recently ranked us at number twenty. Not so great, given our vast wealth, resources, and freedoms.

Any ideas why?

Well, as the book says, there are reasons why people are happy, and it seems that by and large, we are not pursuing those life activities as well as a bunch of other countries. Our emphasis on the material versus the immaterial is certainly one big reason.

Are Americans attempting to medicate away their problems, instead of doing things like focusing on the Laws of Happiness?

If you mean real medicine for depression, for example, then I would say no and yes. Sometimes there are very real biochemical reasons why people need medication, and they could do all of the happiness activities and still have a biochemical problem that needs treatment. So I am all for people taking medicine when appropriate.

But there are a lot of people who do not really have biological problems and would do very well to begin to lead the kinds of lives that produce happiness and well-being. Third, there are the nonbiological clinical syndromes that need treatment as well, but even those would be affected well by doing the activities prescribed in *The Law of Happiness.*

Can you talk a little more about the research that states happiness is 10 percent circumstantial, 50 percent genetic, and 40 percent under your control? This book focuses mainly on the last 40 percent—what encouragement can you give to those whose genetic predisposition toward happiness is less than others?

In some senses, the answer is always to focus on what you can control versus what you can't. And the genetic part is really not that negative for a couple of reasons. First of all, it is very difficult to ascertain what that really means in terms of its effect and also how much we can really alter a predisposition by lifestyle and practices. I personally have seen people who were really not very wired toward happiness get really better as a result of personal and spiritual growth. Plus, if you do have some sort of genetic clinical issue, like depression or bipolar disorder, that can affect mood, that is very, very treatable. So in some senses it is a bit of a red herring in that it gets the discussion going in the wrong direction. The direction we have to focus on is very, very clear: do the things that affect happiness! They are under your control, and even if you were not one of those smiling babies in the hospital nursery, you can be a smiling adult!

You've worked with many high-powered executives and celebrities. Would you say those with fame and fortune are more or less happy than others less renowned or wealthy, and why?

The research is pretty clear about that. Money helps, but not in terms of wealth as much as basic security. If you have attained a level where you are not worrying about basic needs and the things that make life work, the money factor sort of goes away. Really wealthy people do get a tiny bump probably because of some of the ways that their lives can be ordered, but it is not a big deal. The much bigger deal is how they live their lives. If they focus on the things that make people happy, they will be happy, rich, and famous people, and if they don't, you can read about them in the checkout line at the grocery store. There is no shortage of miserable rich and famous people.

Another big factor in this is how rich you are relative to people around you. You can be very wealthy and compare yourself to wealthier people, and then you feel poor and unhappy. By and large, any kinds of social comparisons are a bad idea and rob people of happiness. But in the world of the rich and famous, they tend to do that a lot, and to their own peril.

Your father obviously was a great influence in your life. Who are your other role models?

I was fortunate to grow up in a community with great coaches, teachers, and family friends who all were big influences. And when I became an adult, I was blessed to have had several very important mentors along the way. I still meet with some of them regularly, and they speak into my life. We all need those kinds of influences. But I would have to say, as I wrote about in the book, my dad was the greatest.

Who and what inspires you? What are you currently reading?

I am mostly inspired by good friends and people I know who get up every morning, work hard, and serve the people in their lives well. People who are good spouses and parents, who also do a diligent job every day. The guy who tends to the parking garage at my office building is an example. He is there every day, smiling and serving the people he encounters. Day after day. Or the single parent who is doing the job of two people and making it all work. Those are the people that inspire me.

Currently I am reading some neuroscience perspectives about how the brain develops in the practice of performance and leadership, and also a lot about the need for leaders to be coaches.

What is next in your Secret Things of God series?

Not sure, but after this one, it will have to be some topic that will make us happy!